D0887409

BC

RC 465 .G64
Golann, Stuart E.
 The Bethlehem diaries;
student-mental patient encounters

PC
1.5
G84

5524

The Bethlehem Diaries

Student – Mental Patient Encounters

Stuart Golann
University of Massachusetts, Amherst

Jay M. Pomerantz
Massachusetts Department of Mental Health

Jeffrey Baker
University of Massachusetts, Amherst

Φ *Canfield Press*
San Francisco
A Department of Harper & Row, Publishers, Inc.
New York   Evanston   London

RC
465
.G64

THE BETHLEHEM DIARIES

Student-Mental Patient Encounters

Copyright © 1974 by Stuart Golann, Jay M. Pomerantz, and Jeffrey Baker

Printed in the United States of America. All rights reserved. No part of this book may be used or reproduced in any manner whatsoever without written permission except in the case of brief quotations embodied in critical articles and reviews. For information address Harper & Row, Publishers, Inc., 10 East 53rd Street, New York, New York 10022.

Library of Congress Cataloging in Publication Data

Golann, Stuart E
    The Bethlehem diaries.

    Bibliography: p.
    1. Mental illness--Cases, clinical reports, statistics. 2. Student volunteers in mental health. I. Pomerantz, Jay M., 1939-   joint author. II. Baker, Jeffrey, 1943-   joint author. III. Title.
[DNLM: 1. Mental disorders. WM100 G615b]
RC465.G64   616.8'9'09   74-12420
ISBN 0-06-383030-2

74 75 76 77   10 9 8 7 6 5 4 3 2 1

PREFACE

Many publications discuss and criticize the medical model of mental illness but few, if any, present the patient as seen by the hospital staff, and then juxtapose the patient's view of the hospital. These two perspectives are drawn together by the student-companion diaries, which provide the focus for the book and complete the many-sided picture of the processes of mental illness and institutionalization.

At this time, when the movement away from mental hospitals and back to community care is accelerating, *The Bethlehem Diaries* adds dimension and substantiation to the argument that alternatives to hospitalization are needed. The characterizations and insights that emerge from hospital charts, student diaries, and interviews with patients are far more revealing of the need for community mental health services than are slogans or theoretical arguments. Similarly, the book vividly brings forth the difficulties community alternatives must address.

We wish especially to thank the five students whose diaries are included here, the patients they worked with, and, of course, all the students and patients who have shared in the program since its inception. In addition, the hospital administration participated in and gave their time to program planning and implementation. All names, including that of the hospital and staff, have been changed. Assistant Commissioner George Grosser of the Massachusetts Department of Mental Health supported our work when we called on him.

William Fremouw worked with the project from the outset and was joined soon after by Lewis Breitner and Avraham Frydman. Sheldon Cashdan, Morton Harmatz, Freda Pomerantz, Frieda Rebelsky, Barbara Mainella, Miriam Pratt, and others offered helpful criticism of earlier drafts. Gerald Goodman shared the insights of his own work (1972) with us and made helpful suggestions.

We wish also to thank Darlene Phelan for her help in typing the manuscript. Our special thanks to Sara Ives for her help with manuscript preparation from the book's inception and to Janet Wondra for her dedicated editorial assistance.

S.G.

J.M.P.

J.B.

CONTENTS

The
Bethlehem
Diaries

Student – Mental Patient Encounters

BALLAD OF NEW BETHLEHEM

This is a structure fair
Royally raised.
The pious founders are
Much to be praised
That in such times of need,
When madness doth exceed,
To build this house of bread,
Noble new Bedlam.

Methinks the lawyers may
Consult together
And contribute, for they
Send most men thither;
They put them to much pain
With words that cramp the brain
Till Bedlam's filled with plain-
Tiff and defendant.

Quacking physicians should
Give money freely;
They maculate men's blood
And make them silly
With hydragargyrum pills;
Their reasons and their wills
They ruin, and this fills
Most part of Bedlam.

So good a work as this
Cannot want actors,
But I'll no more insist
On benefactors
But hint such as I see
Hypochondriac be
And are in some degree
Fit for new Bedlam.

I could tell many more
(I have enrolled them)
Should I declare my store
As I have told 'em
With mortar, brick and stone.
Could they their building run
From thence to Islington
'Twould never hold them.

From Thomas D'Urfey's *Wit and Mirth, or Pills to Purge
Melancholy*, London, 1719.

ORIENTATION

FROM BETHLEHEM TO BEDLAM: A HISTORICAL ANALOGY[1]

In the sixteenth century, Henry VIII gave London City
the Bethlehem Asylum for Lunatics. Cromwell, Henry's agent,
had confiscated the hospital along with several hundred
other properties in the campaign to dissolve Catholic
wealth. Prior to that time the hospital had been run as
an asylum by Sisters of Saint Mary of Bethlehem. When
London acquired the building, the Sisters were disen-
franchised as helpers and new support was not provided
for asylum staff or programs. Dialect rendered Bethlehem
Bedlam, overcrowding became a problem, and the asylum was
to become infamous for its fund-raising efforts. From
D'Urfey's "Ballad of New Bethlehem," written on the occasion of Bedlam's removal to new and larger facilities, we
have taken Bethlehem as the name for the New England
state hospital where the events of this book occurred.
The two, Bedlam and our Bethlehem, are analogous in il-

---

[1]This selective history highlights the early years
of the state hospital where this book is set. For a
larger perspective, there are several good accounts of
man's understanding of emotional disturbance, mental
health treatment, and ideology throughout history. The
reader is referred to Foucault (1965), Rosen (1968), and
Zilboorg and Henry (1941).

lustrating how, in all periods of history, mental health programming has been partly rooted in and influenced by the politics of wealth and power and intolerance of differences among people. Henry VIII's actions grew out of the Reformation; the governors of Massachusetts in the 1850s crowded the hospital and decreased funding because they were troubled by pauperism and costs associated with Irish immigration.

THE STATE HOSPITAL AT BETHLEHEM, MASSACHUSETTS

The by-laws of the State Lunatic Hospital at Bethlehem, Massachusetts, published in the 1850s, describe an initial concept of the hospital as a small curative retreat. The superintendent, for example, was expected to "...visit all the patients personally, at least once each day...giving all requisite attention to their medical, moral and physical treatment...." His assistant was expected to "...spend much of his time on the halls, make himself intimately acquainted with the character, peculiarities, and diseases of the several patients, and to exert such favorable moral influence as he can...." But within six weeks of the hospital's opening date, 228 patients were transferred from other state institutions.

Moral treatment is a shorthand term for practices and beliefs including rest, education, diversion, and the undoing of restraints; in the mid-nineteenth century moral treatment was introduced to replace restrictive and punitive treatment of the insane. The history of moral treatment occurred at state hospitals in Massachusetts. In 1887, Butler described the effective use of group meetings and confidential interviews with patients and insisted that institutions could not provide appropriate social influences for more than two hundred patients without suffering a breakdown.

In 1866, at the State Lunatic Hospital at Bethlehem, the Superintendent's Report to the Trustees described many of the assumptions and practices of moral treatment.

If there be principles in accordance with which generalizations may be made and rules formed for the management of the insane, the first and most fundamental is truth. Truthfulness in speech and truthfulness in act should be the primary

motto of him who would succeed in this somewhat
peculiar sphere of life....

The insane generally act from the same mo-
tives and are governed by the same agencies and
influences as other men. If there be any differences, it is that the former, more than the latter, are like children; and the same qualities
which command a ready and cheerful obedience in a
school, which induce order and discipline among
pupils, will effect the same ends in a hospital
and among its inmates. The patients should be
treated as far as possible as if they were not
insane. Treat them like rational beings, and let
them understand that you expect rational conduct
from them, and, with but comparatively few excep-
tions, your expectations are not disappointed.

The road taken by numerous state institutions in
mid-nineteenth century America was that same road taken
to Bedlam in the sixteenth century. In 1863, the first
Superintendent of the Bethlehem Lunatic Hospital wrote in
his report to the trustees, "You are aware that the legislature, at its last session, desirous of reducing the
great expense of foreign pauperism to the State, made a
reduction of thirty-seven cents per week each, in the
rate paid for the support of its insane paupers." He
noted that the hospital population included 246 paupers
and therefore faced a financial problem. He pointed
toward the growing hospital population and accumulation
of incurable cases: "In five years the number of patients in this hospital has increased from two hundred
and twenty to three hundred and eighty-three.... In
all hospitals where no effort is made to exclude them,
the proportion of incurable cases is large and increasing...." Addressing himself perhaps more to the
legislature than to the trustees, he wrote that "...the
problem of a separate, very economical support and management of the incurable pauper insane, that shall at the
same time meet the demands of an enlightened philanthropy,
remains to be solved."

What followed was not a change in philanthropy but a
change in psychiatric ideology from an essentially hopeful humanism to a pessimistic custodialism. Small institutions that had tried to effect re-education and re-
acculturation according to the values of the times became

large and impersonally managed receptacles.

Grob (1966) studied the early history of Massachusetts' Worcester State Hospital and concluded that, "Because psychiatrists were never fully aware of the important part that their own attitudes played in their professional rationale and ideology, they were unprepared to cope with the heterogeneous patient population that accompanied the new urban and industrialized society. Consequently, they were prone to place responsibility for their declining successes elsewhere."

The basic problems of large, minimally supported institutions have remained unchanged even after the dramatic internal improvements in patient management following the introduction of new drugs in the 1950s. In 1961, the Joint Commission on Mental Illness and Health, having studied mental health care in the United States, concluded that "...more than half of the patients in most state hospitals receive no active treatment of any kind designed to improve their mental condition..." (Joint Commission on Mental Illness and Health, 1961, pp. 22-23).

In the last ten years, the mental health field has placed less reliance on large institutions and more upon smaller community-based services. Community mental health is the most recent phase of mental health ideology; the previous ones may be roughly categorized as demonic, moral, medical-scientific, and psychoanalytic. Marked more by service innovations than by theoretical advancement, community mental health represents an incorporation of concepts from public health, such as prevention and planning services designed to benefit a whole community.

Community programs may be organized, for convenience of description, in terms of *new goals* (prevention of emotional disorder), *new helpers* and sources of manpower (college students, as in this book, or teachers), *new services* (among others, consultation or educational programs where mental health specialists attempt to multiply impact by working through community helpers), *new recipient groups* (identifiable groups of people sharing a problem or crisis of mental health significance), *new locations* (such as a general hospital, storefront clinic, or community mental health center), and *new occasions* for intervention (emotional crises or natural transition points like starting school or retiring). In practice, goals, helpers, services, recipients, locations, and occasions are strategically intertwined and community mental health ideology is noteworthy, at least to date, for the degree to which each of these has remained a possible dimension of experimentation (see also Golann and Eisdorfer, 1972). For this particular book, the most relevant experiments involve new helpers, the attempts to develop community alternatives to large institutions, and the integration of the institution into the community by bringing the community to the institution.

THE UNIVERSITY OF MASSACHUSETTS AT AMHERST

During the last decade, while some attempts were being made to reverse the trend toward larger mental hospitals, state institutions of higher learning were growing rapidly. The University of Massachusetts, where the students of this program were attending college, grew in enrollment from 6,495 in 1960 to 20,462 in 1970. Many state universities are essentially urban environments growing in rural areas. Students complain about the impersonality of large dormitory life, the lack of relevance in much academic course work, the grading evaluation procedures linked to graduate or professional school entrance, and the difficulty in finding employment after graduation.

Apart from urbanization on the campus, some remarkable changes were occurring during the decade of the 1960s. The students whose diaries make up much of this book came to the university in 1968 or 1969. Consequently, their first or second year was organized around the student strikes that quickened the politicalization of the campus and the involvement of students in social change both on and off campus. During the past decade one also notes the popularization of experiential learning programs. A few campuses have become known as centers for educational innovation integrating off-campus experiences into the curriculum, but widespread attempts at awarding academic credit for service or practical experience are only now becoming apparent.

The course providing the framework for this book has evolved over the last three years into a two-semester seminar composed of field experience, a consultation-

support group, and a seminar group. The field experience
involves a commitment of approximately one-half day each
week during which each student meets with the same patient, all patients having been chosen from one ward by
the hospital staff. Students do not have direct access
to patients' records.· The students are told that their
role is "counselor-companion," and they know that the patients may be hesitant to meet with them. Priority in
registration is given to seniors and psychology majors
and no other selection criteria are ordinarily used.
There is no attempt to match students and patients except
that same-sex pairings are ordinarily used to expedite
acquaintance and increase the range of possible activities.* Briefly oriented to the hospital in September,
students immediately begin weekly or more frequent visits
which continue until late May. A typical visit lasts one
to two hours.

The consultation-support group is composed of approximately eight undergraduates. A faculty member or graduate student serves as consultant to the group and en-
courages students to raise questions, share anxieties,
uncertainties, frustrations, and other feelings related
to the work they are doing; the group does not ordinarily
discuss individual conflicts and feelings that are not
immediately related to the students' companion experience.
Informal groupings such as those students who travel together back and forth to the hospital also become important sources of support and learning. Members of the
hospital staff serve as resource persons available to
answer questions students may have.

The seminar groups have been organized in different
ways, all attempting to integrate seminar topics, independent readings, and the hospital experience. The seminar as presently conceived attempts to time class discussion topics to coincide with questions and problems
students are likely to be facing. Topics, in order of

---

*Women applicants outnumber men by a ratio of about
two or three to one. That the diaries chosen for this
book are all written by female students is explained in
part by this ratio, and in part by the fact that the
women's diaries were more detailed in their description
of the experience.

presentation, include definitions of deviance, focus on the concept of schizophrenia, intake to the system, the experience of psychiatric hospitalization, the development of mental health policy in the United States, the recognition of mental disorders, and community mental health approaches.

All students in the present program received course credit for their work and many gained a great deal more. When they began their experience in September, 1971, they knew nothing about the patients and little about the institution they would enter. Their experience is captured in their Bethlehem diaries. In the following brief excerpt from one such diary, Kathy anticipates the program's beginning just before her first hospital visit.

September 21, 1971 - Beginning

Meetings and classes twice a week to prepare everyone for what we'll be up against when we finally go to Bethlehem State. I hope someone at the hospital is preparing the patients for what they'll be up against with the students.

Really anxious and restless, can hardly wait for the trip to Bethlehem when I meet my patient. Pretty scared too, though *College Students in a Mental Hospital*[2] has both quelled my fears on one hand and on the other hand made me more nervous. The book and its authors were amazingly professional and yet very much on a student level. *College Students in a Mental Hospital* was written by four Harvard undergrads who participated in the original group of students going to an institution in a supervised university program. Their program took place at Metropolitan State Hospital in Waltham, Massachusetts.

I was particularly interested in their case study program which specifically related to what I'll be doing, working on a one-to-one basis with a patient throughout the year (over two semesters). At the moment the only way I can describe

---

[2] See Umbarger *et al.*, 1962.

my role is that of a *companion*-counselor with
stress on the companion part. But I don't know,
I haven't been there yet and I wonder if I'll
ever be able to come up with a professional definition of my role. I think that it'll probably
be a very nonprofessional people-to-people kind
of relationship. At least that's what I'm hoping.

I expect to learn a lot of things about myself. And hopefully get it together for myself
and my patient.

I hate the word *patient*, can't wait till I
learn her *name*!

Bethlehem State will be my first experience
with mentally ill people, my first time ever in a
mental institution. I'm scared but I need the
experience.

I'm scared because there's so much I want to
do for my (patient) and I'm not sure if I can do
it. I'm scared of failing her, letting her down,
and of disappointing myself.

Unit IV of the hospital, where the events of this
book occurred, serves an area of Massachusetts including
several cities and towns. It has five separate wards,
placed so that the visitor walks sequentially through
them. One enters Ward One off the central rotunda, which
also connects to the outdoors, the canteen, library, and
cafeteria. Ward One is for women who require essentially
no nursing supervision; it is an "open ward"--that is,
the women are free to leave the hospital to go to various
jobs or to walk on the extensive grounds. From Ward One,
one enters Ward Two through a locked door. Ward Two is
for women who require little or moderate nursing care and
they may spend their days in the ward or at various activities in the hospital. Ward Three houses those women
who require closer nursing supervision. It is locked at
all times and it feels much more closed in than Ward Two.
Wards Four and Five are both locked wards, housing men.

The ward physician is in charge of all patients and
is the ultimate authority in a hierarchical system. The
head nurse, who makes the majority of day-to-day decisions
on the ward, reports to him. Weekly staff meetings are
held at which the ward physician, head nurse, other
nurses, social workers, and unit psychologist discuss the

diagnoses, progress, and management of the patients. The
staff of Unit IV is:

Ward Physician:	Thomas Rakosky, M.D.
Unit Head Nurse:	Barbara Olsen, R.N.
Assistant Head Nurse:	Ursula Marra, R.N.
Unit Psychologist:	Sarah Kennedy, M.A.
Social Workers:	Mrs. Louise Meredith
	Mr. Alan Winston
Occupational Therapist:	Mr. Peter Gordon

THE STUDENT-PATIENT EXPERIENCE

In their nine months together students and patients
develop mutually dependent, mutually controlling, meaningful relationships. At entry students experience considerable anxiety and concern, especially in regard to
accepting and being accepted by patients. In contrast,
patients seem to fear ultimate disappointment more than
immediate rejection. Some, having comfortably accepted
the status of mental patient, perhaps view idealistic
students as potential upsetters of their equilibrium;
others may see undergraduate students as insensitive in-
truders, too young and inexperienced to understand their
problems and feelings. Most patients, however, are
lonely, and the students promise to visit them regularly.
Often students enter the experience with barely hidden
fantasies of curing patients; it is possible that some
patients believe students can bring not only relief from
long-felt loneliness, but also relief from long-standing
problems.

For the student the demands of the year, broadly
defined, are to establish trust with a patient, cope with
strong feelings evoked by patient and setting, define responsibility in a confusing and often intense relationship, and test his or her own capacities to understand
and provide support. The patient, meanwhile, has to de-
cide if the student is a source of undemanding social
stimulation and provider of free treats, a person with
whom to talk about problems and feelings, an ally in
gaining desired action from hospital staff, a bridge to
the community and social re-entry, a friend, companion,
intruder, teacher, or substitute parent, sibling, or
child. Patient and student mutually regulate the close-

ness and character of the relationship in response to
on-going feelings and both short- and long-term objectives.

Year's end and the student's imminent departure demand that student and patient reconcile their relationship so as to allow each other existing feelings and
independent directions. This often seems the most difficult task students and patients face in their year together.

The perspectives of professionals and students con-
fronting the lifelong problems of patients differ, as one
might expect. Each comes to the mental patient with his
own expectations and finds confirmation, frustration, and
puzzlement. The patient accommodates to expectations but
at the same time appears unchanging.

In each of five chapters to follow, the reader is
invited to experience the world of the hospitalized mental patient through the eyes of hospital staff, students,
and patients and to share in their actual experiences.
Each of the following case studies has been organized to
facilitate this. The patient's hospital chart, abbrevi-
ated but accurate,[3] is followed first by the student's
diary and second by an interview conducted with the

---

[3]Interviews and diaries are complete and have been
edited only minimally for clarity. All names, including
those of hospital staff, and other identifying information have been changed. The hospital charts had to be
shortened, but we have tried to preserve the quality of
the originals, using footnotes to describe content where
gaps occur. The first chart to appear (Ann's) has been
presented in greatest detail and is intended to be most
representative of the full charts. The complete record
folder on each patient contains an extensive medical history, nurses' records, clothing inventories, often sam-
ples of the patient's letters and other personal and
legal documents, etc., which are not included here for
reasons of space.

The reader of this book, provided with each patient's chart, comes to the patient with a different perspective from that of the student who did not have access
to chart material.

patient approximately nine months after the end of the program. What emerges from a reading of institutional case histories, student diaries, and patient interviews is not a vindication of a professional or nonprofessional paradigm, but a revealing look at the ways they contrast. In Chapter VI we examine in detail the on-going relationships of students and patients over the nine months of their meeting. There is also a glossary of terms and a series of discussion questions for classroom use.

The structure we have chosen to introduce the reader to five cases requires a final word of explanation. Medical charts are sometimes boring, by nature impersonal, and occasionally unkind. Student diaries, in contrast, are often intensely personal and hopeful. Interviews with patients tend to be as revealing as they are frustrating and sad. It is not the authors' goal to reconcile or explain the resulting tension for the reader, but to ask instead that each do this himself. Used in this way the book should prove to be a valuable supplementary textbook in courses concerned with behavior disorder and the psychology or sociology of deviant behavior. It should also be useful in therapeutic companion programs of many types. Most important, it enters the world of mental illness in an unassuming way that we believe has the power to extend the reader's awareness.

1

CAN YOU SHOW ME
THE WAY OUT?

Amy and Ann

"Why Ann and why not me?" are the questions that
puzzle Amy most as she tries to understand Ann's status
as a mental patient and the meaning of the designations
"normal" and "abnormal." Years before, the severity of
Ann's problems might have been more obvious and the reasons for her hospitalization more apparent to Amy.

Ann puzzled the hospital staff in a different way.
The presence of abnormality was never questioned by them,
but her mental illness first was described as psychoneurosis, later as a schizophrenic reaction, and then as
manic-depressive psychosis. The approach used to understand and treat Ann at Bethlehem is typical of mental
hospitals: she was presumed to be suffering from one or
another of the mental illnesses, and the differential
diagnosis was based on symptoms believed to be indicative
of one form of mental illness as opposed to another. The
major forms of psychoneurosis that were described in
psychiatric textbooks of the early 1940s were anxiety,
dissociative, conversion, phobic, obsessive-compulsive,
and depressive, with anxiety believed to be the chief
cause in all cases. The various reactions were thought
to stem from defenses against the experience of anxiety.

The doctors at Bethlehem provisionally decided upon
psychoneurosis, mixed type, as the diagnosis in Ann's case
because she exhibited excessive anxiety in the form of
palpitations, fear of dying, dryness of mouth and throat,

13

and paralysis of the tongue. Furthermore, they considered the initial absence of profound depression, strange
and disordered thinking, or hallucinations. In the eyes
of the hospital staff, it may also have been a more
"hopeful" diagnosis than the subsequent ones in terms of
the course her illness could be expected to follow. When
Ann was hospitalized it was thought that schizophrenia
existed in several forms: simple, paranoid, catatonic,
hebephrenic, and undifferentiated. These were said to be
distinguished by the slow, progressive, undramatic withdrawal of the simple schizophrenic; the fantastic, sys-
tematized delusions of either persecution or grandiosity
of the paranoid; the total negativistic immobility or
extraordinarily dangerous excitement of the catatonic;
the strange, silly, or playful language distortions of
the hebephrenic.

The concept of schizophrenic reaction was a more recent one and implied that schizophrenia emerged partly in
reaction to some traumatic life circumstance. Many symptoms believed to be characteristic of schizophrenic forms
of psychosis are described in the chart: regression, as
shown by not feeding or toileting oneself, grandiose delusions, mutism, negativism, withdrawal, bizarre mannerisms, and reality distortion. In the medical model, diagnosis is presumed to lead to etiological insight, a
greater understanding of the problem's origin or cause.
These diagnostic terms came to be looked upon as explana-
tory rather than descriptive even though they didn't provide the desired insights into the causes of schizophrenia.

Certainly, there are other orientations in psychiatry
and mental health that do not stress illness or concen-
trate on diagnosis of symptoms. Some explore emotions and
ways of defending against them that are either adaptive
or maladaptive, some stress family interrelationships, and
others, learning, reinforcement, and extinction. Some
would deny that mental illness exists in the same sense
as does tuberculosis or other diseases known to clinical
medicine, and would emphasize instead current life problems and response to the experience of hospitalization.
More recently it has been suggested, most notably by
Laing (1967), that the experience psychiatrists call
schizophrenic can be understood as a strategy for living
in an otherwise unlivable situation, and some have moved
so far away from disease as to look upon psychotic exper-

ience as a voyage of discovery from which a more effective personality may emerge.

The reader will find that around 1955, Ann's chart descriptions start to become more positive and, although one might assume that this was a direct consequence of the introduction of new drugs, it would be worthwhile to think about other possible explanations. By the time Amy met Ann in 1971, Ann no longer showed the extreme behaviors that had led to her psychotic designations.

In addition to the great questions of what is normal and what abnormal, and why some people are hospitalized and stay hospitalized while others do not, there are many other issues for the reader to think about in relation to this first chapter. Notice and consider how frequently Ann was transferred from one ward to another; the possible reasons for her improvement and the reasons for her remaining in the hospital after she improved; and, if Amy did not seem to have a significant impact on Ann, try to trace the effects of the experience on Amy by asking what she learned from her year with Ann at Bethlehem State. Notice how at many times Ann and Amy seem to mirror the same issues in each other--particularly issues of dependence and independence, sharing and withholding of feelings. If you had been in Amy's place, how might you have responded differently?

BETHLEHEM STATE HOSPITAL

MEDICAL RECORD

Ann Janik[1]   Patient #52841

MENTAL SUMMARY - APRIL 12, 1939

HISTORY   The patient is a twenty-seven-year-old
female, married at twenty and now separated, the
mother of three children. Her married life was
stormy and unhappy almost from the beginning,
her husband drinking to excess, suspicious of
her fidelity, and frequently threatening her
life. She separated from him in May, 1935, and
went to live in her sister's house. In August,
1935, her husband came to the house while intox-
icated and beat the patient about the face and
hands as well as injuring her sister seriously.
He was arrested after that and served three
years in jail.

    At about the same time that her marital
difficulties reached their peak, patient complained of pains in her left chest and saw a
number of doctors all of whom informed her there
was nothing wrong with her heart, that it was
all nervousness. Her chief complaints were
pains in her left chest, palpitation, dryness of
the mouth, and fear of impending death. Patient
also had been considerably upset by her relationship with Mrs. Bell of the Employment Office,
who she states had a number of times mentioned
that she should be sent to the hospital and had
accused her of being a dope fiend. During the
few weeks prior to her commitment here she ate
and slept poorly and lost about thirteen pounds.
She became so nervous at home that her parents
finally decided to have her sent to this hospi-

---

[1]Ann was admitted to the hospital on April 6, 1939.
The first entry in her chart describing her family history and background shows the same date. Several days
later, the routine Mental Summary was entered.

16

tal for care and treatment.

GENERAL APPEARANCE   Patient is a twenty-seven-year-old Polish female in pack, moaning and groaning. Her facial expression is at times blank and staring with the pupils of her eyes widely dilated. At such times, patient is inaccessible and it is difficult to get her attention. Suddenly she will become very agitated and repeat in a stereotyped manner, "I know what it is all about."

ATTITUDE   On admission, this patient's outstanding symptom was her emotional lability. Some of the time she would be cheerful and calm and then suddenly she would become excited and complain of heart palpitation, dryness of the mouth, etc. She managed to make a fairly good adjustment here until after she had received a typhoid innoculation on April 10, when she again became tense, apprehensive, anxious, and fearful. She gradually became so disturbed that it was necessary to transfer her to hydrotherapy for wet sheet packs. Since the transfer, she has been extremely disturbed, uncooperative, and this morning assaulted one of the nurses.

AFFECTIVITY   Has been variable. There were periods shortly after admission when she showed perfectly normal affect and then quite suddenly, without any apparent cause, she would become depressed, agitated, and fearful. This is her condition at the present time.

FLOW OF THOUGHT   There have been occasions during the past few days when the patient seemed completely withdrawn from her environment and would stare fixedly ahead as though in reaction to false sensory perceptions. At such times, the examiner would receive no response to questions. Today she showed the same sort of reaction on occasion, but when she did speak, she would talk in a voluble, rambling manner with a tendency to repeat certain phrases, among them, "I know what it is all about. Oh, we're going up in the air...please...don't do this...I know what it is all about...oh, my God...I can't

breathe...I know what it's all about...they are
taking me up in the air."

    Q. How long have you been here?

    A. I will admit it. Quite some time. I
        know what it's all about....Oh, I
        want to get well, but it seems as
        though I can't.

ORIENTATION   Patient is oriented as to person
and place. Repeated efforts to determine
whether or not the patient knew the date were
without success.

MEMORY   Could not be tested because of patient's
lack of cooperation. Patient shows no evidence
of mental deterioration so far as the examiner
can observe.

GENERAL INTELLIGENCE   Patient attended public
school, repeating only the eighth grade and
leaving school at the age of fifteen. She does
not impress the examiner as being mentally deficient and therefore a psychometric examination
was not requested. In her present mentally disturbed stage, she could not be tested.

JUDGMENT   Patient appears to have partial insight when she admits that she is mentally sick.
"I know I am sick. They are taking pictures of
me to see the sickness I have got. I admit it.
I have had a nervous breakdown." Today patient,
for the first time, expressed a number of delusional ideas. She is definitely suspicious of
the examiner and the nurses, today assaulting a
nurse. "Please don't do this to me anymore. I
can't stand it. I was hypnotized. Eleanor
started this. I know what it's all about. She
just passed me...oh, minstrel show...I know what
it's all about. Let the nurses do what they
want. I just want to be laid to rest. They've
got me now. I know what they want to do to me.
Please don't...oh, yes, I remember." As will be
seen from above, the patient entertains a variety of delusions, chiefly of a persecutory
nature.

PERCEPTIONS   This patient looks and acts hallucinated. Some of her productions today appeared to be in response to what she heard. Statements made by other patients on her ward, she refers to herself. On one occasion she admitted to the examiner that she was usually unsuccessful in her attempts to determine exactly what she heard said.

OTHER PSYCHOPATHOLOGICAL MANIFESTATIONS   This patient has probably been unstable and nervous at least since her separation from her husband in May, 1935, and she has lived in constant fear that her husband would return to kill her since the episode in August, 1935. She has exhibited the common symptoms of psychoneurosis, including palpitation, dryness of the mouth and throat, "paralysis" of the tongue, and the fear of death from heart disease. Although the examiner has not had the opportunity to discuss sexual matters with the patient, he is convinced that there has been much sex conflict. When she becomes somewhat more comfortable mentally, this subject will be more thoroughly investigated.

DIAGNOSTIC IMPRESSIONS   The diagnosis in this case must be provisional. The examiner prefers to lay emphasis on her psychoneurotic symptoms because they have existed for a much longer period of time and, therefore, diagnoses the case provisionally as Psychoneurosis, Mixed Type.

RECOMMENDATIONS   Hydrotherapy, psychotherapy, and when improved, recreational and occupational therapy.

JUNE 4, 1939[2]   This patient has been cared for in hydrotherapy for the past few weeks where she is mute, negativistic, resistive--shows a fixed, staring gaze and blank expressionless face. According to the nurse, she refuses to visit with her company when they come. She soils her bed,

---

[2]Entries in Ann's chart during the twelve years from 1939 to 1951 picture her behavior as deteriorating and presenting difficulties in management to hospital staff.

but lately has been taking a satisfactory amount of nourishment so that tube feedings are no longer required.

For a time after her admission, this patient impressed the examiner as being a severe Psychoneurosis, but at the present time she has all the earmarks of a Schizophrenic Reaction.

JULY 28, 1939   Transferred to make room.

JULY 30, 1939   Transferred to make room.

AUGUST 24, 1939   Patient was transferred to hydro because she had been somewhat disturbing, especially at night. When we saw her on the ward, she was standing quite rigidly with head back, mumbling under her breath short phrases which appeared to rhyme, but which we could not make out. Her legs were edematous and cyanotic. Shortly after she arrived at the hydro, she suddenly broke out loudly with the following: "I am President and Treasurer of the U.S. of America. I am now President and I am to be taken out the front door and to Washington as I am to settle the fate of the world. That certain person is to meet me at that front door and take me to confer with Roosevelt who is now Vice-President. . . .My birthday date is to be on all calendars of America, as I am President. I am to have the special date and go through the Golden Gate. This certain person will go with me as a guard. I am trying to save the world. All the struggle he has risen, now he must go into prison. All the world is turning late, all the world is turning hate. Tara is also to be taken in to prison with his wife as they have ruined my life. There is water, fire all over the world."

SEPTEMBER 21, 1939   Today this patient's condition was again one of catatonic stupor. She lay in bed with her eyes closed, completely withdrawn from her environment. She was extremely mute and showed some negativism and resistiveness when the examiner attempted to raise her arm.

JULY 14, 1940   The patient continues to be cared for on Ward Three where she has been lying on her bed verbalizing in the manner described in the previous notes....There are several abrasions on her face which she picks at. She appears to be a case of Schizophrenia, probably Mixed Type.

JULY 16, 1940   Transferred to make room.

NOVEMBER 1, 1940   Transferred. Improved.

JANUARY 5, 1941   Transferred. Improved.

JANUARY 11, 1941   ...There is no change in her condition.

AUGUST 29, 1942   Transferred. Readjustment.

NOVEMBER 5, 1942   This patient has a rather blank expression on her face. When questioned, she mutters unintelligible sounds. On the ward, she sits quietly all day. She is very untidy in her habits and has to be toileted regularly. Undoubtedly, this patient has deteriorated mentally. The original diagnosis is not appropriate at the present time. The diagnosis now is more of a Schizophrenic Reaction. The possibility of a Perplexed Manic must also be considered. Electric shock treatments might be of benefit.

NOVEMBER 6, 1942   Transferred from E-1. Denudative in tunnel on way to cafeteria.

JANUARY 9, 1944[3] She appears to be quite deteriorated, shows a mannerism of crossing one finger over the other. She allows her fingers to be straightened out, but within a few minutes they are found to be crossed again. She does not speak when spoken to. She requires a good

---

[3]There were no chart entries during 1943.

deal of nursing care.

JUNE 30, 1944   Transferred to make room.

AUGUST 11, 1944   Transferred to make room.

AUGUST 24, 1944   Transferred to make room for someone else.

JANUARY 27, 1946[4]   She is untidy even when toileted. She is assaultive, impulsive, destructive, and noisy. She is very manneristic and does not speak when spoken to.

JUNE 10, 1946   Transferred. Blocking toilets-- needs closer supervision.

APRIL 25, 1948   At the time of admission, this patient was considered a Manic-Depressive; however, she has been getting quite untidy and is apparently deteriorating. She has never had electric shock treatments and possibly she might benefit by some and the series was started on this date.

MAY 30, 1948   She has received a series of ten electric shock treatments without noticeable improvement and they were therefore discontinued on this date.

OCTOBER 1, 1948   She is frequently assaultive and consequently is kept separate from the group, usually in one of the guarded, unlocked rooms. She is muted and today would not reply to any questions put to her....The nurses believe that she is overaffectionate as she is frequently seen sitting on the lap of another patient when she is in the group.

---

[4]There were no chart entries during 1945, two as included above during 1946, and one in 1947 which was essentially the same as the last 1946 entry.

JANUARY 16, 1949   Transferred. Assaultive and resistive. Better classification.*

JANUARY 2, 1950   Transferred. Improving.

FEBRUARY 28, 1950   Transferred, very untidy. Better classification.

JULY 1, 1950   ...The attendant reports that the patient is cooperative or assaultive according to her whims--that she was frequently in seclusion--and that the description of her behavior as noted above is characteristic. No change.

JULY 5, 1950   Transferred. Very assaultive recently.

OCTOBER 1, 1950   Transferred. Doing a little better.

OCTOBER 14, 1950   Transferred. Better classification. More untidy and disturbed.

JUNE 8, 1955   ANNUAL NOTE   "...she is not interested in her personal appearance. She is not cooperative, is assaultive. She is disoriented in all spheres. She is deluded--thinks she is pregnant. Her flow of thoughts is incoherent with flight of ideas. Hallucinations are not elicited. Memory is bad. Judgement impaired and she has no insight. She eats and sleeps well. Patient is on combined Thorazine and Serpasil."

OCTOBER 7, 1955   This patient attended four sessions of group psychotherapy during the month

---

*Better classification in this context means a different ward placement more appropriate to the patient's level of psychopathology, cooperativeness, and independence.

of September.[5]

FEBRUARY 2, 1958   Patient has been extremely persistent in demanding that social service locate her husband, have him arrested for nonsupport, force him to come to the hospital to take her out, find out if he obtained a divorce and re-married, etc. The superintendent was consulted and advised that contacting husband would not be in the best interests of either husband or patient.

FEBRUARY 28, 1960[6]   Letter to husband returned marked "Not here." She was also advised that earlier social service efforts to locate her husband have been unproductive. The efforts

---

[5]During 1951, there was one chart entry which showed no change from previous descriptions, and the next chart entry was in 1955.

During 1957, the patient left the hospital for weekends and longer periods in care of her sister and returned seven times. For most of this time, her condition was described as improved, and she was maintained on drugs.

In 1958, the patient began efforts to locate her husband and numerous chart entries reflect this. She was also issued a privileged I.D. card.

[6]There are no chart entries during 1959, but entries of 1960 and 1961 indicate that she intensified efforts to locate her husband, devoting much of her time and energy to this.

The next entry is in March, 1962, at which point she is again described as untidy, regressed, and needing closer management. However, by July of the same year, she is described as neat, tidy, interested in her appearance, neither assaultive nor destructive, and doing better. The pattern of improvement and relapse continued during 1962 and 1963. During this same time period and in subsequent years, the patient and social service continued in attempts to locate the patient's husband and arrange for alternative placement for her. During 1964 and 1965, chart entries reflect these attempts.

were made by mail.

JUNE 1, 1965   ...Social services helped this
patient on many occasions, but could not help
her locate her husband nor could they find any
other resource to help patient financially.
However, in 1961, she was transferred to a re-
habilitation ward, improved very much in her appearance and mannerisms, and worked in the
sewing room several hours a day for several
months. She continued to be cooperative and
able to participate in ward activities, had parole, got along well with the other patients.
Her memory had improved and it was very good,
but her judgement remained impaired.

    Patient was taken by worker to visit sever-
al rest homes. Several weeks after this trip
visiting rest homes, patient began to regress
and stated that she had changed her mind about
going into the community. She refused to have
worker contact her relatives and stated she did
not want any part of them nor did she want them
to know she was being released from the hospital. During the months that followed in 1963
and 1964, patient managed to manipulate a transfer to many other wards, withdrew from group activities, and preferred to have no contact with
the worker. Patient stated that she was afraid
to go out into the community, that she did not
feel well enough, and wanted to be transferred
because of some commotion that had been going on
in the ward. There were certain patients the
patient did not get along with and according to
the ward personnel, patient became very talkative and disturbed at times and her behavior was
quite bizarre.

    In March of 1965, patient requested her own
transfer because she felt she could not stand
the patients on present ward. Her latest request is that she wants to know under what section she has been committed, what it stands for,
and what she has been doing here for twenty-five
years. Worker will visit patient on ward, clar-
ify this with the patient, and discontinue all

intensive work with the patient. Worker feels
that this patient certainly is not a good candi-
date for placement due to the fact that she cannot remain stable long enough to adjust to community living.

APRIL 2, 1969   PROGRESS NOTE[7]   This slightly
obese female patient, who was seen on the ward,
is neat, cooperative, coherent, and fully oriented. However, she seems a bit depressed and
complains that her family doesn't visit her at
all. She is neither assaultive nor destructive,
and she mingles with the other patients and often participates in their activities. Her insight into her condition is quite good; however,
she is a chronic complainer. At the time she
was seen, she listed a number of somatic complaints. Patient's present medications are
Artane and Mellaril.

SEPTEMBER 28, 1969   Transferred--reason: unitization.

---

[7]There were no chart entries for 1966. All six
chart entries of 1967 note transfers from one ward to
another. The year 1968 is described as one of physical
illness and complaints and numerous medical diagnostic
tests are described in the chart. Entries during 1970
and 1971 reflect further physical problems, and trial
placements on open wards. At times, she is described
as much improved, but at other times, the chart reports
her to be agitated and delusional. The last entry before
the time that Amy began to meet with Ann reads, "Transferred. Patient has improved. May now again be tried on
an open ward."

AMY'S BETHLEHEM DIARY

First Day - Introduction

Impressions:
Expected to see younger patients.
Expected to see violent behavior, extreme withdrawal, etc.
Found most patients "begging" (silently) for attention--seemed to need personal contact and attention more than anything else.
Expected to be rejected at first, and then gradually accepted.
Found Ann to be extremely excited and more than willing to see me.

October 5 - First Visit

I arrived ten minutes late and Ann didn't think I was coming. I immediately had her make a collage but she was hesitant at first. She didn't know what a collage was. She asked my opinion about what pictures to use and how to rip them out effectively. She wanted me to glue the pictures in place because she would get messed up. I showed her a neat way to glue the pictures and gently made it apparent that I wanted her to finish the collage. After it was done she felt quite pleased with herself and hung it on the wall.

I then suggested we go for a walk since she said she walked two hours twice a day and had missed her morning walk. She was extremely talkative and told me some startling things about herself. She said she had been in the hospital for thirty-two years, the first two years in a "wet pack" in a solitary cell. Instead of feeling bitter about this experience, she was thankful, saying that the hospital saved her life. Otherwise she would surely have committed suicide.

For ten years Ann has had parole and she enjoys the freedom. She said she didn't know what she would have done in "there" without it. I never knew what those privileges entailed. The other years when she was locked up, she said she was too sick to do anything or go anywhere.

Ann is very hopeful that she will get transferred to a rest home. I talked to the social worker and Ann is indeed qualified to go into a rest home but red tape and financial matters are holding her up. Ann has expressed the fear that her daughter will not sign the release. She said, "My daughters have nothing to do with me." She later said that when she was committed, at the age of twenty-seven, she left her three children with her sister.

Ann said that she was in the hospital because she never got over something that happened to her a long time ago. She now attributes her condition to a physical illness and not a mental illness. It was her nerves that gave her a "nervous breakdown," not a "mental breakdown." Ann also went to great lengths to point out a woman who was committed for drowning her three children. I feel there is some connection between Ann's case and the woman's. I don't think Ann hurt her children, at least not badly, but I think she might have wanted to and feels bad about her desire.

Ann is extremely worried about lack of money and is hopeful the hospital will make her husband buy her a new coat--she said her last one was a donation. She said he had not bought her anything in thirty-two years, and fifty dollars isn't going to kill him.

Ann doesn't like to do things. Her main activity is going for a walk or taking a shower. She is terrified of pills (yellow ones that make her throat dry so she can't swallow) and operations or bodily injury that is fatal. She made two references to freak accidents, one in which a woman died of a dislocated shoulder--she had a heart ailment; and a man whose tonsils froze and his whole neck became immobilized and he lost consciousness. Ann also mentioned a broken ankle and told me about the "something" that knocked her out so she wouldn't feel pain. She was proud that she didn't get sick as everyone thought she would.

Ann's two favorite programs (the only ones she watches) are "The Lawrence Welk Show" and "The Dating Game!"

Ann and I had times when we didn't know what to say to each other. I found that the topic of food interests her and she is trying very hard to diet. I am a food science major so we have a lot in common on that point.

At 4:30 p.m., I left, relieved that I could drive away and then remembered that she couldn't, and hadn't for the past thirty-two years.

October 12

I got a ride over with Sara and Kathy and didn't know they were only staying for an hour and a half. I guess I'll drive alone from now on because I would like to stay with Ann for about two and one-half hours. I felt really bad when I had to explain to Ann why I was leaving so early.

Ann seemed extremely happy that day. Someone had just taught her how to play cards and she wanted to play with me. It was a good sign as Ann doesn't usually like to do anything.

Ann was also happy because she had won at bingo three times and she wanted to go into town to spend her winnings. I thought she knew we had to take a taxi but when I asked her where we could call one she was really shocked. It seems one of the other inmates goes in her volunteer's car and Ann assumed she was going in mine. After Ann realized we were going to take a taxi she didn't want to go.

Ann expressed the need to get in touch with a certain doctor because her husband was supposed to have been in court this past week. She wanted to know how the case went--if it went in her favor, she would receive some money. As Ann and I sat down to play cards she showed me the front page of a newspaper which she had been saving for me. The article she wanted me to read was about a boy who was killed in a motorcycle accident. This was not a particular hit with me because one of my boyfriend's good friends was killed riding one last summer. Ann noticed my silence and didn't know what she had done--in fact, the article mentioned my friend's death.

After I won at cards a few times I had to suggest another game. I didn't mean to win, in fact I tried my hardest to lose--I dropped certain cards I wanted her to ask for and skipped my turn a few times. Ann was hurt when she lost but I tried my best to let her win.

Next we played monopoly. I made sure Ann won. She seemed to like that game well enough, but she complained because it was too "hard." After a while, though, she caught on.

Our session went all right, but if I could have stayed longer it would have been a lot better. Also, I should have made sure I had enough money with me to take Ann shopping in town, and maybe to have bought her an ice cream or something. As it was, I only had a dollar in my wallet, just enough for the taxi. I also shouldn't have let her see me get upset about the newspaper article.

It did seem odd, though, that Ann should show me the article because our conversation previously had nothing to do with accidents or death or anything that could remotely be associated with the paper. I still feel that Ann is too preoccupied with physical harm. I would really like to know why.

October 19

Nothing much happened today. Ann and I just played cards and talked about her leaving the hospital. She is particularly anxious about her husband's court decision.

Other than discussing her future and playing cards, the session was uneventful.

Oh yes, Ann shows an unusual interest in other patients' behavior and whether or not they are following the rules. It is a tattletale kind of an attitude.

October 26

Ann and I went into town. The trip was very uneventful. She looked mostly at clothes and couldn't believe how expensive they were, though we were looking in Woolworth's and other tacky shops. This just emphasized for me how poor Ann is. I also felt a little guilty about my own background, as my family is fairly well off.

After about an hour in town, Ann and I were bored so we went back. I was struck by the fact that Ann and I were probably taken for mother and daughter while we were shopping. I felt funny about this as I didn't want a "crazy person" to be associated with my mother-figure. This was a gut feeling but I was able to cover it up in my mind and relax for the rest of the trip. I guess I felt that way because I used to have serious doubts about my mother's sanity and Ann just brought back some unpleasant feelings.

After Ann and I got back to the hospital we played fish. Ann is extremely good at this and we had a good time. An hour later I left. Ann seemed happy that she had gone out shopping.

November 2

This was a monumental session for me. Up until today I had never asked Ann any personal questions about anything she had not first brought up. If she wanted to talk about something, fine. If she didn't, o.k. I figured that even if she never talked to me about things that bothered her, I would be accomplishing something just by showing up every week and being her friend--someone who would share activities with her and make her feel as if she could be an interesting person.

Well, today Ann told me that Roberta's patient was afraid to talk to Roberta because she was afraid Roberta would ask her questions about why she was here, etc. Ann also said that a lot of the patients were afraid of this-- afraid they would have to reveal part of them that they didn't want to talk about. I quickly reassured Ann that Roberta had no such intentions, figuring that Ann might say something to Roberta's patient.

Later, Ann and I were out on a walk, and Ann again mentioned the subject of volunteers questioning patients. I realized the first time that Ann was telling me this specifically because I had asked her no questions and she thought I was somehow "different" from some of the others (as she believed they were). Knowing that Ann wanted to know why I didn't ask questions, I told her that I didn't care why a patient was in the hospital, all I cared about was if she improved or not. I also told her that I was learning a great deal by coming to see her and that I

liked coming. I told her I would still like to come even
if I never knew anything about her past. If she wanted
to tell me--fine--if she didn't--fine--I would still be
there because I liked her and I was learning something.

A few minutes later, Ann told me she was put in the
hospital by mistake because she couldn't breathe, but
also added, "I would have ended up here eventually anyway." At least she admitted that she did have a problem
at one time. Ann also told me a little about what happened the day she was committed.

I guess Ann revealed some of this information to me
because I told her that the hospital thought she was
ready to· leave and that only financial matters were
holding her up. Ann was very happy that the hospital had
recognized her behavior as "good," in compliance with the
rules.

The welfare board is going to review Ann's case tomorrow. If they approve some money, Ann can get out very
soon. If not, the hospital will pay and she will go on
family relief. Either way, Ann will be getting out.

I forgot something else of importance. Ann is for-
ever complaining about other patients' behavior and how
they don't take their medicine or they leave the T.V. on
after ten o'clock, etc. She always says, "If I did that,
I'd be on the closed ward so fast, but with them it's
different." I asked her why she didn't tell the nurses
if someone really disturbed her. She immediately said
that she would never tell on someone else because the
nurses would put her on the locked ward for making a pest
of herself. Every time I came, however, she would have
someone new to complain about.

During our walk today, we saw another patient who
was out walking without permission. This happened to be
the same patient that Ann had complained about earlier.
Ann couldn't see why this other patient could get away
with everything while she, Ann, couldn't do anything.
I let the subject drop thinking Ann was just fed up with
the place and was dying to get out, away from the arbitrary rules.

As we walked into the building, however, Ann stopped
a group of nurses walking out and told on the patient who
was walking without permission. Afterwards, Ann looked

very pleased with herself. When we got to the ward, Ann
again denounced the patient's activities and re-emphasized
the fact that it wasn't fair.

November 9

The impossible just happened. Ann got put on the
locked ward for arguing with another patient at 4:00 a.m.
She is only supposed to be locked up for one or two
weeks--until she "calms down." I was so mad I didn't
know what to say to her. Ann is a model patient in that
she doesn't refuse her medicine, hit other patients, or
take parole without permission.

Ann told me she didn't want me to visit her anymore.
I told her "too bad because I'm coming anyway." I told
her if she didn't want to talk to me that was o.k., but
that I would be at the hospital every Tuesday afternoon.
Ann repeated again, however, that she didn't want me to
visit her.

Ann also said she had no desire to move back onto
the open ward. If she was going to keep getting put back
on the locked ward, it wasn't worth it. She felt it
wasn't fair that no one else was put on the locked ward,
just her.

Ann seriously feels that she is not being treated
like the other patients. She isn't getting out of the
hospital as quickly as they are, she gets locked up when
they don't, etc., etc. I am having a hard time consoling
her because I, too, feel that Ann is really getting the
short end of everything. She's been there for so long
with no money and no one to fight for her that she is
literally forgotten.

I went to see Mrs. Olsen about Ann and told her I
didn't think Ann should have been transferred. She said
Ann had "pulled this thing before" and that they were
only putting her on the locked ward to quiet her down.
I asked what exactly Ann got punished for. Mrs. Olsen
said she complained too much about the other patients.
After patiently pointing out that otherwise Ann was a
model patient and that complaining about other patients
was relatively minor, Mrs. Olsen and I compromised. I
told her if they would let Ann back onto the open ward

after a maximum of a week, I'd talk to her about not bugging the nurses with complaints. Mrs. Olsen agreed to this.

My next task was to tell Ann. This was hard for me to do because I felt Ann hadn't done anything wrong and that in reality Ann was acting as any normal person would. Needless to say, Ann did not take my criticism lightly. She yelled back at me and told me it wasn't fair. It was great! Ann was taking out some of her hostility on me. After she calmed down I told her I didn't agree with the nurses but that she had to play this "game" if she wanted to go back to the open ward. Ann then declared that she never wanted to go back to that ward and that I needn't come to visit her.

I left, reassuring her I would come again.

November 10

I was really worried about Ann, so I went to see her again today. She said she didn't want to see me and that she would go straight to the nursing home from the locked ward. I told Ann that I wouldn't leave, that I had some chemistry homework to do. I guess Ann figured that if I was going to stay there at all, I was going to talk to her. Anyway, she kept on telling me she didn't want to see me, but she got a chair to sit down in and started talking to me. I asked her if she wanted to play cards but she said no. After about fifteen minutes, I asked her again and she agreed. As usual, we played fish.

Things looked pretty good when I left. Ann looked much happier and she seemed to understand what I was telling her about "playing the game" in order to get out of the hospital.

November 16

Went to see Ann and she was still locked up. Really angry, I went to see Mrs. Olsen but found out she was on vacation, so I talked to one of the nurses instead. She told me Ann was supposed to leave the ward but the board voted against it, saying Ann wasn't ready yet. "What constitutes being ready?" I asked. The nurse then said Ann had refused to take her medicine and that she looked upset. I promptly replied that Ann's medicine was so strong it made her sick, and that she was unhappy because she was locked up. The nurse looked as if she was going to throw me out of the ward any second, so I made a hasty retreat and paid Mrs. Meredith a visit.

Mrs. Meredith didn't even know why Ann was moved over to the next ward. I carefully explained what had happened, biasing the story by emphasizing Ann's point of view. After all, I figured if I didn't, no one would. Mrs. Meredith jotted something down and then I left. I felt that Mrs. Meredith was going to work on something although my hopes aren't up too high.

I didn't actually see Ann too much because it took so long running around looking for Mrs. Olsen who was on vacation. Ann and I did talk about a few things, her needing a coat, a pair of shoes, etc., but not much happened. She did say that she appreciated my talking to the nurse and Mrs. Meredith. I guess that's good.

November 23

I was sick and couldn't see Ann. In fact, I couldn't see her all week, as whatever I had was highly contagious.

November 30

Ann looked a lot happier when I went to see her. We played monopoly a little, and a lot of cards. She was much happier since she was moved to the open ward again. I noticed she did very little complaining about other patients. I don't know if she was afraid to, or if she listened to what I had to say.

I am beginning to realize that Ann and I are getting along pretty well. We are always happy to see each other and we feel relaxed in each other's company. I don't know if this happened just recently or if it has been happening for a while and I just haven't noticed it. I've noticed the same thing with Kathy and Sara, two other students. Sally and Robin look at me searchingly as

I walk in the building. They want to know if *their* volunteers are coming too. I get the feeling that we really
mean something to these people. It must be so terrible
to be locked up without being allowed any of the things
we take for granted.

Things have been happening in the Thursday discussion
groups, too. Either Dr. Katz is changing or I'm getting
used to him. At first I couldn't stand him and felt funny saying anything around him. I felt that he was the
"shrink" and I was someone stupid. I thought he was
going to jump on me any minute for saying something that
was without purpose. After Sara said that he was different from us because he didn't have a patient, I began to
see things in a new light. I realized he was there to
round out the group, and to act as an advisor. It was
the fact that he didn't have a patient which made him a
good person to listen. It gave the group an added something it would never have had. I also feel that I can
tell him to be quiet if I want to and that some things he
says are bullshit (although they never are). I guess
that he is less of a Ph.D. and more one of us.

I also feel that the group is really getting close
except for the few who never say anything.

December 7

Ann and I did the usual. We talked and played cards
and I told her about my friends getting busted. She's
very much concerned about not having a coat and about
taking too much medicine. Nothing of any real interest
occurred.

December 14

I took Ann out in my car. We went looking for a
coat and some dresses but found nothing. Then, I took
her for a ride around the university. I showed her my
dorm and offered to take her inside, but she didn't want
to go. She didn't say much but she seemed to be enjoying
herself. She met two of my friends who were hitchhiking
and seemed relieved that I didn't introduce her as "Ann
from Bethlehem." In fact, she seemed very excited about

meeting some of my friends.

Ann surprised me by giving me a Christmas card. It really made me feel good.

December 18

Three of my friends and I decided to stop in and visit Ann. It really made me feel good to see her face light up as we walked in. Knowing how much she loves to play cards, I set up a game of fish; my friends are also card lovers. We played for about two hours and Ann won, which made her really happy. She also obviously loved the attention she was getting. I hadn't told her I planned to visit but I called just before I left to make sure she'd be in. The nurse told her that her social worker was coming to visit her (I don't know where she got that one), but Ann said she figured it was me. I guess it pleased me that Ann thought I was the kind of person who would make surprise visits.

December 20

I sent Ann a Christmas card and called to tell her I was sick. I hope she wasn't too disappointed.

January 4

Went to see Ann today. She was obviously happy to see me although she was very unhappy with Mrs. Meredith. I guess Mrs. Meredith was supposed to do some work on the case, but hadn't done anything. I offered to talk to Mrs. Meredith, and Ann really wanted me to. I waited outside Mrs. Meredith's door for twenty minutes. I "got the eye" from just about every male patient who went by which made me feel terrible. I didn't want to let them know how much their advances disgusted me, but I didn't want to encourage anything either. Then I thought about how horny those guys must be and how the females at Bethlehem are so unfulfilling that it must be hard for them not to look at anyone new.

I finally got to see Mrs. Meredith. She said Ann

talked about my coming to visit her and that it was obvious Ann liked me a lot. I assured her the feeling was
mutual. She made it obvious that she hadn't been working
on Ann's case, so as tactfully as possible, I made it
clear that I was going to bother her every Tuesday until
something is done. Mrs. Meredith said Ann was going to
be suggested for one of three openings at a new halfway
house opening up in Eastboro and I told her I thought
that was a terrific idea and a good thing for Ann. Mrs.
Meredith then asked me if I would be seeing Ann if she
moved to Eastboro. I assured her I would and told her
I had my own car. I even hinted that I might see Ann
next year. That seemed to be a big point in Ann's favor.
Mrs. Meredith then said she was definitely "going to work
on it." I took that to mean I would be seeing Mrs.
Meredith again next Tuesday!

Ann told me she never got my message about being
sick. I was really surprised because the hospital had
given Ann a previous message from me. Ann also told me
that Sara had left a message for Sally, and Sally never
got that message either. I don't know if a new nurse is
taking the calls or what, but it's a pretty inefficient
way to run a hospital. Ann and Mary waited for us and
didn't know why we failed to show up.

Not much else happened. Ann and I played cards and
she gave me some perfume.

February 10 - New Semester

I haven't had my notebook for a while and I'm sitting in the cafeteria eating my lunch, looking back at
past events and trying to sort out some feelings. I went
to the Thursday discussion section today and started
thinking back to September. When Ellen told us the story
about the volunteer who thought Ellen was a patient, I
tried to remember if I was patronizing towards Ann. I
didn't think I was but I reread my diary just to make
sure. Much to my relief, I wasn't a mindless jellyfish
who was trying to spread good will to all those poor deprived creatures in the mental hospital, but just a plain
old scared college student who was prepared for any shock
that might be coming.

I've changed a lot since September. I guess I've grown up a little. I'm beginning to feel that my life has direction and that I'm becoming an individual. I've separated from Michael and I've decided to live my own life. I look at Ann and realize she really can't branch out and grow--she kind of died thirty-two years ago, and probably even long before that. When I go and visit her it's like my life is beginning and hers is coming to a slow halt. The people in the hospital are existing but not living. I don't know what I'm writing or why I'm writing it. I guess I'm trying to say that Ann and the whole hospital experience has really affected me. After seeing people whose life potentials are cut off, it's easy for you to make damn sure that the same thing does not happen to you. I shouldn't say easy, but it makes you realize what you've got and how much can be taken away.

I've also made a lot of friends because of this hospital program. There's something binding about a group of people with a common interest and a semicommon goal. I say semicommon because no one really can define our goal, although I expect we have more or less the same expectations or desires concerning our roles in the hospital.

I also feel that I mean something to a terribly lonely and forgotten old woman. It's a weird feeling knowing you're the only person that someone else can rely on. I guess it's a lot of responsibility. If we were cruel enough, or stupid enough, we could really screw up someone's mind.

On to better thoughts--it looks like the other social worker, Mr. Winston, is going to take over Ann's case. Maybe something will happen.

Ann and I haven't talked much about intellectual pursuits or true confessions of yesteryear, but we chat about how bad the food is and how cold the weather is, how great my apartment is, and how rough my exam is. It really doesn't matter what we talk about because we're pretty comfortable with one another. We play cards a lot, and I'm working on getting her to say she wants to go to the rest home. I know she does, but she won't say it because she's afraid of getting let down. I don't

blame her either but if she says she wants to go loudly
enough, maybe Mr. Winston will work harder on her case.
I guess anything's worth trying.

February 14

Saw Ann again today. She was waiting by the window
and saw me pull up in my car. I guess she really looks
forward to these visits. Her back hurt and she was really down about her medicine but we played cards and I
talked to her about my apartment.

She talked about a new patient who was admitted just
recently. I guess anyone new really shakes them up--they
want to know where she is from, what's wrong with her,
etc. Ann seems really involved with the other patients--
that's all she talks about--how much so-and-so bothers
her and how the nurses treat "Sally" differently from her
and how it's not fair. Sometimes I think she talks about
the other patients simply because she has nothing else to
say--there's nothing else she can talk about.

She had a new dress on today; it looked very nice on
her although she didn't like it because it was too short--
it came to the middle of her knee. I just thought, "God,
I don't think I own a normal length dress."

I left and Ann seemed really sad to see me go. I
knew I should have stayed longer but I was really bored
and thought about my physics exam coming up. The hospital's o.k. for about an hour, and then it turns into a
depressing place to be.

February 21

Was really sick today, so didn't see Ann.

February 29

Didn't see Ann at all last week as I had strep and
did not want to give it to her. It was nice seeing her
this week and I think we kind of missed each other. Ann
complained about her back and the fact that she couldn't

go to the bathroom. She looked sick--she didn't want to
move and she wasn't playing cards well at all. She was
throwing out any old card and letting me win.

She told me a friend of hers who didn't know she was
in Bethlehem had written. I asked how the friend knew
where to write--she said, "Oh, I saw her name and address
in the obituary column when her husband died so I wrote
to her." Ann also told me that her daughters had told
this friend that she was dead. I guess that must have
made Ann feel terrible because I know she really cares
about her daughters and feels guilty about having left
them.

It's morbid that Ann would look through the obituary
column and write to people she knew. I don't know if she
has a sick mind and likes doing morbid things like that
or if communication with the people she knew is possible
only by waiting for one of their relatives to die.

I left feeling kind of down and Ann was feeling bad.
I was depressed about things that were happening to me so
together we made a great pair.

March 6

Was really depressed before I went to see Ann. All
sorts of really bad things are happening to me socially.
I started dating other people for the first time in two
and one-half years and my dating experiences were really
terrible. I can't believe there are so many messed-up
people in the world. Instead of Ann's being locked up,
I have a couple of candidates.

I walked into the ward and Ann looked pretty happy
which cheered me up a little. One of her cousins came to
Bethlehem to visit a relative of Ann's and found Ann ac-
cidentally. The cousin promised to come back again so
Ann really feels as if there's someone else in the world
who knows she's alive.

She said she felt a lot better and we played our
usual game of fish. I hate the game but Ann doesn't want
to learn any other card games. Today I brought in Pokeno,
a playing card bingo game. I thought Ann might like it
because she used to play bingo a lot. She didn't like it,

however. I guess that's because she didn't win all the
time (even though I deliberately left spaces uncovered so
she would). It really bugs me that Ann won't play anything unless it's easy and she wins all the time, but
I've been playing cards since I was six so I've had lots
of experience. I want to treat her like a woman but I
don't want her to get upset when she loses. I compromise
with myself and let her win sometimes and try to win other times--in fish, that is. I would always win if I
didn't cheat a little, and then Ann and I would have one
less game to play.

I really wanted to talk to Ann about my bad experiences dating but she hasn't gone out with anyone in
thirty-two years and her marriage was really lousy to begin with. It would be great if I could ask advice but I
can't. In that sense I am a very real part of the active
world. I am confronted with all of its problems and com-
plexities but Ann is isolated and unable to experience
the things I am experiencing. Probably she can't remember her experiences when she was my age.

Ann is from Westmont and has *never* been outside of
Westmont except for rare one-hour trips to other parts of
the state. I was born in England, I've traveled all
over Europe alone and I've gone to California, Florida,
Canada, etc. I've always had freedom and I've never been
happy sitting and doing nothing. Ann is happy that way,
so it would be hard for me to tell her I want to get a
Ph.D. and do research, and that I don't want to get married, but I think living with people when you're not married is o.k., or that I smoke grass and live in a coed
dorm where everyone is super close and we do everything
together. I know she would never understand that, so I
haven't even bothered to tell her. I don't know if
that's right or not. I've just acted like a nice little
girl around her. Maybe I shouldn't--maybe I should, I
don't know.

Well, I have to continue this next week, my friends
just came over.

March 13

Really short session. Vacation is coming up and

I've got an awful lot of exams. I was pretty happy today.
I had a good weekend and things are looking better, although they are still not terrific. I told Ann I wanted
to go skiing this vacation. She looked really depressed
and said, "Does that mean you won't be seeing me that
week?" I told her that if I went I wouldn't see her but
I'd only be gone a week. She asked me if I was excited
about going skiing in Canada. I told her I was but that
I'd been to Canada before. She really couldn't understand
what any other place was like.

We played cards and made small talk. Nothing really
happened and I left pretty early because I had a lot of
studying to do.

March 20

Vacation is almost here and things are tense although
I'm happier than I have been for a long time. I'm really
getting close to one of my friends. It's weird. He
thinks he's really messed up and he uses his hangups or
problems as an excuse not to have strong relationships
with people. Being close and spending time with him makes
me wonder "what is normal" and why is Ann there and he
here. He thinks he is messed up and Ann thinks she isn't
but one is locked up and the other has his own self-
imposed prison. I find myself wondering what are the
criteria for becoming a mental patient. Is it that Ann
is more obviously socially deviant or unwanted than my
friend is, or is everything arbitrary? Sometimes I think
that no one is sane anymore--but then I consider myself
to be different from a mad rapist or an insane killer.
But there are other people whom I don't consider myself
to be different from. I'm more outgoing, I say socially
acceptable things and follow many of society's rules,
breaking them only quietly. But I still have the same
hangups everyone else has. I want to be loved and needed.
I want to feel that my life is being fulfilled somehow.
I feel that many of the people in Bethlehem are just like
me but something went wrong along the way. Maybe they
were always made to feel worthless and were convinced nobody cared, but that's not being crazy--that's being incomplete. Sometimes I wish I had a machine that would
give everyone the vital feelings that they were missing

so that no one would have to be labeled a social deviant or a crazy person. Life can be really beautiful if you have enough strength and self-confidence to get through many of its ugly parts.

Back to Ann. We had a pretty boring session. I wasn't thinking about what she had to say. I was just looking at all the other patients and saying to myself-- why them--doesn't anyone want them? I left not remembering much about the afternoon except that I was glad to get out of there.

March 27

Saw Ann because I didn't go skiing. At the last minute no one wanted to go with me. It turned out for the better because I was pretty broke.

Ann and I talked about little things. She told me about Susan going shopping with Sarah and how it wasn't fair that she couldn't go with me.

I told Ann I was going on a twenty-mile bike ride. She said, "Don't you dare--I won't let you--that's dangerous!" Talk about keeling over in surprise! I immediately told her it was o.k. and that I would take care of myself. I also gently hinted that I was an adult and that bike riding was fun.

I talked about going to summer school and about the little Italian restaurant where I would be working. I also told her I wanted to travel across the country. She seemed surprised but wasn't nearly as alarmed about my going cross-country as she was about my going bike riding.

She said she wanted to go shopping as soon as she felt better. I told her that any time she wanted to was fine with me.

I left feeling kind of sad and wondering what the hell I was doing there. I know she enjoys seeing me and looks forward to it but I often wonder if I'm doing enough or if I'm doing as much as I can with our relationship.

Well, I don't want to think I haven't done a good job, so I'll sign off now before I really start to analyze everything.   Otherwise I'll never get any other work done.

March 30

    Went to discussion section for the first time in a
month.   I hadn't gone because I was sick for two Thursdays, one Thursday I mixed up and forgot that we were
going to Bethlehem so I missed the rides, and the last
Thursday I was too depressed to go to any classes.
Things were really getting me down that day.

April 3

    Ann and I talked about the nursing home and she re-
ally doesn't want to go.   I think that in some strange
way she thinks she is getting back at Mrs. Meredith for
not letting her go earlier.   I feel bad because I know
Ann will have more freedom and better medical attention
in the nursing home.   She'll be able to go downtown whenever she wants to, too.   She's really afraid of being
sent back to the locked ward if she does anything wrong
and it's hard for me to tell her that she can't do anything "wrong," that she's a woman who should be able to
do what she pleases as an adult.   No hospital should have
a hold on someone as peaceable as Ann.   She only verbally
attacks people, not physically.   Anyway, she's determined
not to go to the nursing home and loves it when nurses,
etc., try to convince her to go.   She feels as if she's
getting her own way for the first time but it's only by
depriving herself of something that might be beneficial
to her.

    The rest of the session was very superficial and
quite routine.   However, she did point out a few choice
pieces in the obituary column, which I'm growing used to.
I can change the subject after saying, "Oh, that's too
bad," very nonchalantly.   Maybe someday she'll be more
interested in the living.

April 10

    I'm really happy.   I just got accepted into an hon-

orary fraternity and things seem to be going really well.
Walked into Bethlehem in great spirits.

Ann and I walked around the grounds. It's the first
time she's been outside in a long time and although we
didn't talk about much, I really didn't think we had to.
Ann and I are comfortable enough with each other that si-
lences aren't awkward any more. I brought her a geranium
from home and she really liked it. I think it made her
feel good to take care of something and water it.

When we got in from the walk we played cards for a
while and then she told me her husband tried to kill her.
She showed me the scars, saying he also tried to kill her
mother. He supposely went to jail for two years and was
let out. After that he got a job and never communicated
with his family. The kids went to live with Ann's sister
and I guess Ann lived there too for a while. Three years
later she said she had a nervous breakdown because she
knew her husband was getting out and she was afraid he
would kill her. I didn't know how much of this story to
believe but I'm pretty sure there is a basis for truth in
what she says. It's weird, it *could* happen. Someone
would go to Bethlehem for a "nervous breakdown" and never
come out because she exhibited peculiar habits--as maybe
Ann did. It seems like something right out of Rod
Serling's Night Gallery.

I left in pretty good spirits. It was really great
having Ann tell me her story because I felt trusted.
Whether or not it is true doesn't matter--I think she believes it's true and it is an important part of her life.

April 17

It's a holiday today and I forgot to go and see Ann.
I couldn't believe I forgot. All weekend I kept on
thinking Saturday was Friday and so on. I didn't know
what I was going to tell her. I thought of all sorts of
fantastic excuses but then I decided to tell her the
truth.

April 18 - The Truth

I walked over to Ann and said hello. I told her

I forgot to go yesterday and that I was sorry. It was
o.k., she said. She figured I did forget. I felt really
good knowing I hadn't lied although it's a small point--
it meant something to me anyway.

The rest of the afternoon was quite routine. I left
feeling a little guilty but happy.

April 24

Ann seemed happy to get out when we went for a walk.
I brought one of my kittens over and Ann let it cuddle up
to her. I asked her if she wanted it, but she said no
because it would be too much bother and all of the other
patients would be petting it. I told her if she changed
her mind, the offer was still open.

We played cards and Mr. Winston came up to us while
we were playing and said, "Ann, I have a proposition for
you. There's an empty room in the Petersfield Nursing
Home."

Ann said she didn't want to go anymore, and that,
"you should have let me go when I wanted to go."

Mr. Winston immediately said to *me*, "Yes, Ann's upset because she was put on Ward Three after that little
incident." He went on talking to me as if Ann weren't
there and I had a tremendous hold on her or something.
In effect, he asked me to convince her to leave. I ignored him in irritation because he talked about Ann as if
she were a child. He wouldn't even talk to her--that's
how low an opinion he had of her as a person.

After he left I again mentioned the fact that she'd
have more freedom in a rest home, but Ann was firm. She
didn't want to go. I really didn't blame her either.
For the first time it really sank in about why she didn't
want to go. I decided to leave her alone and let her
stick to her own decision. If she's happy at Bethlehem
then it's her life and her decision.

I've found that I can accept Ann as a person more
than I could before, but that person is not a real person
by my standards. To me she is lazy, bossy, opinionated,
catty, gossipy, unmotivated, and generally quite a bore
to be with. On the other hand, she is lonely, very con-

siderate of me, she's reliable, friendly, and very open.
I know if I had to live with her I'd go crazy--but seeing
her once a week is o.k. However, if I was in this program again next year, I don't know if our relationship
could grow anymore. I doubt it. Ann and I are too different to have anything but a superficial friendship.
It's a warm friendship--but it's a limited one.

May 1

     I had to go to the bank at the same time I was sup-
posed to see Ann so I went to the hospital to tell her
I'd be late. Her immediate reaction was, "Can I go with
you?" I said sure, we could do something to get around
the rule, but she immediately gave up and said, "No, I'd
better not." It was really sad. I felt as if Ann were a
little kid who couldn't break any of the rules--otherwise
she'd be punished.

     I came back an hour later, we took a walk, played
cards, and talked for the second time about my leaving.
She seemed to be taking it pretty well, but I know it
really hasn't sunk in yet.

     I have never been so bored with her as I have been
today. I left as soon as I could and went back to my
apartment and took a long nap.

May 5

     It was Ann's birthday today and I bought her a box
of chocolates, wrapping them up in bright paper. She did
not expect me so when I knocked on her door she was really surprised. I had to leave right away because I had to
pick up my brother--but I was happy I got her something.

May 9

     Couldn't see Ann yesterday because I had to go out
of state to pick up my brother's dead car. Ann said she
didn't get my message until three (I was supposed to be
there at two), although she didn't seem to mind too much
and was really happy to see me. We played cards for a

long time and I wasn't as bored as I have been. I stayed
longer than usual, rapping about little things and she
said she wanted to go downtown to shop next time I saw
her. She wanted to go this week but I told her I couldn't
because I had a lot of work to do.

I know I'm going to miss her and it's hard for me to
think that I'll see her two more times and that's all.

I tried talking about my personal life to Ann but she
didn't want to listen. I get the feeling that she wants
to forget I have a life apart from the time I spend with
her.

Not much else happened, it was a pretty routine
session.

ANN JANIK

FOLLOW-UP INTERVIEW[8]

JP - Do you have a student this year?

    No.

JP - Do you remember your student?

    Amy Scott.

JP - How did you get along?

    Very good. We went down the street a
    few times. She took me out to the uni-
    versity once. She bought me a box of
    chocolates for my birthday; also a ge-
    ranium plant. When she came here we
    used to play cards mostly. She had a
    car of her own. But then the nurse or
    somebody else said that we could not go
    in the students' cars. It is against
    the insurance policy of the state. We
    took a taxi a couple of times after
    that.

JP - Did you learn anything from her?

    She taught me to play a few card games.
    We also went for walks on the grounds.

JP - Did you like her?

    She's nice. A smart girl. She's in
    her last year at the university, but
    she's taking another course so she
    couldn't have me this year.

JP - Did she learn anything about you?

    She told me that they had a meeting
    every week, on Thursdays, at the uni-
    versity where they tried to learn more
    about us. She also told me about her
    brother and her home life.

---

[8]All follow-up interviews were conducted by Jay
Pomerantz (JP).

JP - How come she told you that?

> We were just talking about things.
> Once she told me how she used to ride
> her brother's bicycle.

JP - How come she's not in the hospital but you
are?

> She's studying to be somebody....She's
> a well person....I'm here because I had
> a nervous breakdown.

JP - But you look pretty calm?

> She's a small person, very easy going.
> She almost always wore trousers.

JP - I thought I said that you looked calm.

> Oh, thank you. Maybe because I'm
> taking medicine.

JP - Do you miss her?

> Yes, I do. She came up to see me late
> last fall. Just once after she came
> back to school.

JP - What did you talk about?

> I was planning to go to a rest home and
> she went down to Mrs. Meredith to see
> about it....She's rented an apartment
> with three or four other girls plus a
> cat for company.

JP - Ever tell her much about yourself?

> I spoke with her about myself.

JP - What kinds of things?

> What happened that caused me to come in
> here.

JP - How did she take that?

> She didn't say much but was always in-
> terested in me. Oh yes, and a few
> times she brought me in cakes.

JP - Is what you told her, the things that happened to you, kind of sad?

Yes, they were.

JP - How did she take that?

She felt sorry for me, the things I've
been through. She used to correspond
with me, too, from her home.

JP - How close did you get to her?

Just as a friend.

JP - Do you have many friends?

Yes, too many!

JP - What do you mean?

They're always pestering me with their
troubles or their advice. Ann do this,
Ann do that. I don't always care to
listen to them.

JP - Was it that way with Amy also?

Yes.

JP - Can you tell me more about that?

She didn't speak too much about her
private life.

JP - I bet you kind of felt she was getting more
from you than you were getting from her?

Yes.

JP - Is that the way it is with all your relationships?

No.

JP - I get the feeling you didn't find Amy a
great deal of help?

Well, we played cards mostly.

JP - You mean you were willing to talk more but
she didn't seem to want to listen?

No. She didn't pry much into my private life.

JP - But that's kind of where your trouble is?

Yea.

JP - What would have happened if you really told
     her all your troubles?

> Be the same thing. I'd still be here.

JP - You mean you didn't see her as someone who
     could be helpful?

> Well, I've been here so many years. No
> home or anything. Now going to meetings
> about a private rest home. But I'm not
> going to bother with it. I'm on three
> different kinds of medicine.

JP - How is it that you ended up in this place?

> I got up one morning and couldn't swal-
> low. Called the police. Thought they'd
> give me oxygen or something. Instead
> brought me here and I've been here
> thirty-two years.

JP - You could have left, couldn't you?

> Yes, I could have before.

JP - How come you stayed?

> Well, Mrs. Meredith was supposed to
> call my daughter but my daughter never
> called back. Also, the welfare didn't
> want to pay for my board at the rest
> home. They did for the other patients,
> but wouldn't for me.

JP - Is that the way it is with you? You get
     the short end of the deal all the time?

> Yes.

JP - Got anybody in the world you're close to?

> Just my sister and her husband.

JP - That's not too many people.

> No. Well, my mother and father are
> dead. I'm pretty well along in years.
> I've three daughters but I don't have
> anything to do with them.

JP - How come?

> My daughter wouldn't tell me where my

husband was. One of them was even
living in the same town with him. Another patient finally had to tell me
where he lived.

JP - How come your daughters are like that?

They are on my husband's side. He
tried to kill me and my sister and I
never got over it. He belongs here,
not me. Instead he's got a job for
the past twenty-five years. His family
always been here at Bethlehem, not mine.
His family, two of them died here. His
whole family is peculiar. Russian people, not Polish.

(Interruption - patient leaves to get her medicine)

JP - So he tried to kill you?

If I hadn't gotten away from him, I'd
be a dead person today.

JP - But why didn't you just separate from him?

I was separated from him. I was living
up at my sister's, staying away from
him and minding my own business. He
came up there after me.

JP - But I don't understand why you'd end up
here for thirty-two years.

Well, years ago things were different.
I spent sixteen years on a closed ward.
I worked all the time, at least twenty-
six of the thirty-two years. They liked
to keep good workers here. Years ago
that was the policy. I also spent two
years in cold pack--that was a treatment
they gave to you years ago. Well, all
those sixteen years I didn't see my family. I didn't know nothing about them.
If I hadn't located them through a social worker, I'd not know where they are
today. I guess my family wanted me to
stay here all my life and forget about
me.

JP - And what's your reaction to all this?

> You get used to everything. I haven't
> seen anybody from home in twelve years.

JP - Do you think the hospital is better now
than it used to be?

> Oh, yea. Much better.

JP - In what way?

> You get to have a room of your own. I
> also have my own assignment work and I
> have parole.

JP - You think the hospital made people sicker?

> No. Now with the new medicine and
> things, lots of people have improved
> and gotten out of here.

JP - Take the difference between you and Amy.
You think she will have the kind of life
you had?

> She's happy. She has friends and has
> a nice house and a mother and father.

JP - You put first the fact that she's happy?

> Yes.

JP - You think that's the important thing?

> Yes.

JP - How come you ended up so unhappy?

> I don't know. I never did anything to
> anybody. I don't understand why I
> should be given the kind of life I had.

(Goes to see what time it is)

> I got it better than some people though.
> I can go on parole alone or with a part-
> ner--all over the grounds. Whatever
> I've got, I've gotten by hard work.

JP - You no longer seem to expect much?

> I don't feel well enough to go to a rest
> home. Other people singing and talking

out of their head or talking to the
wall or putting their finger up in the
air for nothing and they rarely have to
take one pill. I don't do nothing to
nobody and have to take three different
pills. Been taking medicine close to
thirty-two years and I've had about
enough of it.

JP - Did you used to look forward to Amy's
visits?

Yes.

JP - Did you think she learned anything about
mental illness from you?

We never talked much about it.

JP - It seems like being here has become a way
of life for you.

Just like in a mill, the same old daily
grind every day.

JP - Is it better than the way life was before
you came here?

No, I was happy at home.

JP - You mean with your husband?

No, I was at Sister's house. Me and
the three children.

JP - Didn't fight too hard, did you?

I tried as hard as I could. Went out
weekends two years to my daughter's
mother-in-law's house. But she didn't
have a home of her own and didn't sign
me out. Then she stopped coming.

JP - So people start and stop with you?

They don't care nothing about you.
Only look out for themselves.

JP - Aren't you the same way?

No, I've done a lot for people and the
hospital too. I have even tied shoes
for nurses and rubbed their backs. You

think I'd do that now? No sir. Not
the way they kept me here.

JP - Why did you do those things for the nurses?

They asked me to.

JP - If I asked you to jump out the window,
would you do it?

No.

JP - Is that part of your troubles?

Always too good to everybody and never
did anything for myself.

JP - Is that why you married your husband--out
of pity for him?

No, I loved him so I got married to him.

JP - Do you feel you gave more to Amy than you
got back?

No, I liked her friendship.

JP - How come you didn't have a student this
year?

I like to lie down in the afternoon.
I get up at 5:30 a.m. and then the other patients keep the T.V. on at night
so late it's hard to sleep. I have to
have my rest.

JP - Didn't want to start and then have to stop
with someone else?

No.

JP - Or was it you hoped Amy would come back?

I thought maybe she'd come back this
year.

JP - You kind of like relationships you already
got going. Don't like the process of
starting new ones?

That's right.

JP - You think it's a good idea, the idea of
having students come to the hospital?

Yes.

JP - How come patients themselves don't talk
more to one another? Why do we kind of
have to import people into the hospital
to get conversation going?

Lots of times because the patients are
sick, on a lot of medication. They're
liable to hit you if they don't like
what you say.

JP - But it's not that way with the students?

No.

JP - What about with the hospital staff?

They're all right. Nobody bothers you.

JP - But the hospital staff kind of has control
of your life.

Yea.

JP - Get lonely sometimes?

I take one day at a time and let it
pass.

JP - Not too much fun though?

No.

JP - I guess it's almost time for lunch. Thanks
for talking with me. By the way, do you
know if Jane Frank is still here?

She's not. They let her go to a rest
home--twenty-eight years old. Never
worked a day in her life and they let
her go. I'm sixty-one, worked thirty-
two years here and the nurse says I'm
too old to go!

JP - Thanks again. Can you show me the way out?

Yes.

2

I CALLED HER
MY GUARDIAN ANGEL

Ellen and Mary

What are the characteristics of total institutions and what effects do they have on persons who live or work in them? According to sociologist Erving Goffman (1961), the key feature of total institutions is their bureaucratic organization designed to handle the many human needs shared by whole blocks of people. The basic arrangement of modern society is such that people sleep, play, and work in different places with a different set of persons in each place, and without an overall rational plan. Goffman writes that

> The central feature of total institutions can be described as a breakdown of the barriers ordinarily separating these three spheres of life. First, all aspects of life are conducted in the same place and under the same single authority. Second, each phase of the member's daily activity is carried on in the immediate company of a large batch of others, all of whom are treated alike and required to do the same thing together. Third, all phases of the day's activities are tightly scheduled, with one activity leading at a prearranged time into the next, the whole sequence of activities being imposed from above by a system of explicit formal rulings and a body of officials. Finally, the various enforced activities are brought together into a single rational

plan purportedly designed to fulfill the official
aims of the institution (p. 6).

Ellen's major concerns during her year at Bethlehem
included the effects of institutional life and practices
on the patient and upon the attitudes of "outsiders" toward "insiders." During her year at Bethlehem, ideas
Ellen had previously learned in her courses--for example,
how being in an institution reinforces dependency--took
on new and fuller meaning. Notice how she was able to
extend her ideas further through hard introspection and
speculate why people living in institutions may begin to
feel that other people are against them.

Notice as you read how Ellen was able to learn and
generalize from insights into herself, into the student-
patient and patient-hospital interactions, and into
Mary's interpersonal style, or "games" as Ellen calls
them; then notice how Mary experienced the same events
differently from Ellen, and try to get a feeling for the
dynamics of the give-and-take between them. Finally, try
to note the sequence of phases the relationship went
through, and how both Ellen's and Mary's feelings and
expectations changed during the year.

BETHLEHEM STATE HOSPITAL

MEDICAL RECORD

Mary Kristine   Patient #64220

ADMISSION NOTE[1]

This patient was admitted July 19, 1956, at 9:20 p.m. She was brought to the hospital by her husband, accompanied by the sheriff, M. Olim.

According to the admission papers, "Gradually gets more depressed, and has been considering suicide." This is the first admission of this twenty-nine-year-old, well-developed, fairly nourished, married, white woman, who is untidy in her appearance and whose feet are dirty. Her affect is inappropriate. She showed evidence of being depressed, but at times smiles inappropriately. She expressed her guilt feelings for telling so many lies, stealing coats from stores, and for having sexual relations. Her husband is cruel to her and they are not compatible sexually. She admitted having suicidal ideas. Patient was cooperative with the admission procedure. She was oriented in all spheres and was able to give all of the statistical information necessary for admission. Her memory for remote and recent events seemed good. Delusions could be elicited: she states that she lost God and that people are always talking about her. She admitted hearing voices, but did not want to say what the voices were telling her.

AUGUST 10, 1956   DIAGNOSTIC IMPRESSION   ...this reaction came on when this woman, whose social standing in marriage had been below the level of other members of her family, had been taunted by

---

[1]Mary was admitted to Bethlehem State on five different occasions prior to the time that Ellen started working with her. Her first admission was on July 19, 1956.

them because she had not succeeded as well as
they had. She has been made to feel quite
guilty about her lot....Add to this the patient's having a husband who is not too understanding, and whose goals are not too high. The
patient has always felt a need to compensate for
feelings of inferiority by trying to have other
people see her in a better light....All this
adds up to a pretty disturbed woman with little
reality satisfaction and to whom everything
seems frustrating.

I would be inclined to say that this woman
is suffering from a Psychotic Depressive Reaction, rather than an actual Schizophrenic Reaction, based on her severe guilt feelings and
also on the nature of her course in the hospital.[2]

ADMISSION NOTE - MARCH 5, 1957

This patient was admitted at 12:45 p.m.
She was brought to the hospital by a police of-
ficer at the request of her husband who was unable to leave his job. Patient comes in on voluntary, desirous of entering the hospital. This
girl has had a lot of difficulties, has numerous
guilt feelings and, actually, things have not
been easy for her. Apparently, she has been
building up tension during the past four to
eight weeks and voluntarily reported to an outpatient clinic....However, she has been upset,
her delusional thinking has caught up with her,
and she has started to worry again. This morning she became acutely disturbed, crying, sob-
bing, and then suddenly pacing around in a very
agitated manner and not talking at all, to the
point where the neighbors were informed by the

---

[2]After continued improvement in her general ward behavior and a number of successful weekend visits home,
Mary was discharged in January, 1957, and treatment was
continued through the outpatient department. The second
admission occurred the following March.

girl to call the husband. He asked if somebody
could not bring her back to the hospital. On
returning here, patient seemed oriented to where
she was, recognized me and some of the nurses,
but refused to say a word and would only shake
her head in answer to questions....She would not
talk to give the information, but seemed quite
aware of the fact that she is ill and needs help.
She cried a great deal, shook, looked somewhat
run-down physically, seemed definitely to be
begging for help, and apparently was having this
delusional thinking, which was upsetting her.[3]

DECEMBER 17, 1957   Patient is still very unhappy about her marriage and more determined to get
a divorce. She says that she has an appointment
with her lawyer, whom she is going to see after
the interview. She saw him last January for the
first time. This time her husband is going with
her. She says her husband is now going along
with the idea of divorce, which he formerly ignored. She does a lot of ruminating about the
past, thinks that her marriage was all right
while her mother-in-law was alive; the patient
depended on her, and since her death, has been
in difficulty. Now the hospital gives her a
measure of protection against her husband who
refrains from physical abuse. She described her
husband's cruel treatment of her son, how he
picked him up by the coat collar and threw him
against the wall, just because he was in a hurry,
forgot his hat, and returned to the house for it.
She talks about her children with motherly con-

---

[3]The majority of entries during the two years subsequent to this admission note weekend visits, with Mary
leaving the hospital in the custody of her husband. Typ-
ically, her condition was described as improved, although
in some entries increased symptoms were noted. During
this period the chart entries describe her as preoccupied
with her marital problems and with resentment towards her
husband, children, and another man. The December 17,
1957, chart note is typical of those describing her second admission.

cern and says that she would go without food to see that they had what they needed....

MARCH 24, 1958   This patient received a total of ten electroshock treatments, the series having been concluded on March 10. She became quite confused on these, and now two weeks following their completion is showing considerable improvement. Her memory is returning, she is becoming interested in the home activities, and went out for a day during this week and made out very well....[4]

ADMISSION NOTE - JANUARY 12, 1962

This thirty-five-year-old married woman, accompanied by her husband, was admitted voluntarily at 3:20 a.m. today. According to the husband, the patient has been depressed and hallucinating. She has delusional ideas that her seven-year-old daughter will become blind and crippled. She attempted suicide by slashing her throat and both wrists shortly before she was admitted here.

On admission, the patient appeared depressed, withdrawn, preoccupied, and somewhat confused. She admitted hearing voices, but did not elaborate on it. She said that she worried very much about her daughter who is going to be blind and crippled. In fact, she worried so much that she wanted to die....

FEBRUARY 15, 1962   Condition - Improved. Visit home in care of husband. Much improved, without psychotic symptoms, but she is a hostile person.

AUGUST 21, 1962   Reported from visit with husband. Condition is still fair. She is clean

---

[4]Chart entries for the next year report outpatient visits. During this time, she lived at home, medication was maintained, and the status of her concerns remained as noted above. Mary's third admission was on January 12, 1962.

and in good nutritional condition. She is, however, unhappy and seems to be building up some
tension. Children have been ill, and she has
been tormented by anxieties. Recently her husband struck her during one of her panics. She
cried about this. Husband corroborated this.
Evidently, he is lacking understanding. Her
conversation is coherent and not delusional.
Given an appointment about one month later, as
she is very unstable and needs support.

ADMISSION NOTE - FEBRUARY 14, 1967

This forty-year-old married female patient
was admitted today for the fourth time at 10:15
a.m. on voluntary. She came from home and was
accompanied to the hospital by her husband. Patient is rather short, hyposthenic, and slim.
Her hair is light brown, she is edentulous, and
wears glasses. She appears tired, tense, restless, and depressed. At times, she laughs inappropriately and is preoccupied by her own
thoughts.

Patient complains of tiredness, tension,
and depression. Also she said that she does not
sleep well and her appetite is poor. Her speech
was monotonous and she was overtalkative. She
had flight of ideas and she expressed guilty
feelings for things she has done in the past.
She said, "I made my mistakes." She showed me
the marks on her wrists and throat and told me
that she had attempted suicide in the past. She
said that recently she thought of suicide. She
complains about her way of living, and she said,
"I don't get out much. I take care of my six
children. My husband is always working. He
gives me thirty dollars a week, but this is not
enough. I was thinking of getting a divorce,
but I have nice children," etc. Later she said
that she gets along well with her husband. Sub-
sequently, she expressed unconnected thoughts:
"I don't know how to read well the Bible. I always worry about nothing. My husband says I am
impossible to get along with."

Patient was well oriented in all three spheres. Her memory was satisfactory. Her general knowledge was fair. Judgment at this time is impaired, and her mind is cloudy. Intelligence cannot be evaluated at this time. Patient said that she went to school until the tenth grade. Patient at this time is depressed, bizarre, and uneasy. When here before she was classified as Schizophrenic Reaction, Chronic Undifferentiated Type. She was placed on Thorazine and Stelazine.[5]

JULY 8, 1969   Reported from visit with husband. Patient was well dressed and neat. Said she feels better since she gained some weight. Says her mind is o.k. and her husband says, "She has been perfect." As the prescription was being written for her, she launched into a long history of all her troubles. Husband says these are true. It seems that all her realistic troubles have given her a very sour outlook. She says, "On June 21, I will be married twenty-five years. We probably won't go out to celebrate and all I have to show for these years are six children." Concern over dilapidated furniture and money problems. Denies suicidal thought; she says, "I must live for my children." Husband advised to take her out more and to report in three months.

ADMISSION NOTE - SEPTEMBER 15, 1970

This is the fifth admission to Bethlehem State Hospital of this forty-three-year-old

---

[5]The subsequent two years of this chart again note a series of weekend visits lengthening into more extended periods of absence from the hospital and then outpatient visits with the patient living at home. Some of the entries reporting on her condition out of the hospital indicate improvement and the absence of severe tension or hallucinations, while others reflect their return. The last entry of the fourth admission was in 1969.

married Protestant female, who enters the hospital this time under Section 42, voluntary care.
On admission, she exhibited a smiling facial expression, although occasionally she would cry.
She says that she has "something wrong" in her
mind.   She talks about having frequent daydreams.
She thinks that she is dangerous and has a tendency to kill people.

She is oriented in all spheres; memory
seems to be intact.   Medication is Stelazine,
Mellaril.   Tentative Diagnosis: Schizophrenic
Reaction, Chronic Undifferentiated Type.

ELLEN'S BETHLEHEM DIARY

October 6

I hope I'm not being overly optimistic but things went well today. I'd only met Mary for a brief few minutes when we went on our orientation tour of the hospital--and she seemed very depressed at the time but not "emotionally disturbed." This second time was different. She really did seem "out of it"...but I think she was interested in me and I think she felt accepted--that's why I'm optimistic.

I'd brought a deck of cards because I was afraid we'd have nothing to discuss. But Mary talked quite a bit, usually about her family, and how she'd ruined her life, etc. The reason she seemed "out of it" to me was that she constantly referred to "the mind reader in Westbridge" who knew all about her and how it would soon "all come out"; how no one wanted to associate with her because of "what she'd done."

I'm pretty sure she was testing me for sincerity, for trustworthiness. One resolve I made by the day's end was to try to be a genuine person. Down to earth, sincere. The reason I think she was testing me and the reason I decided to be genuine is this: every so often during the hour, she'd begin to cry and lament about ruining her life. My natural impulse was to try to comfort her. At one point, we had this conversation (approximately): Mary (crying), "My whole past has been a failure...no one likes me." Me (I spoke quickly--I was reacting to what she said and my goal was to "give her a new slant"), "Sometimes it's better to look toward the future and forget about the past--that's over and done with...and *I like you*." (I meant it.) Mary: "You're using psychology." She kept crying.

She seemed to be saying I was only saying I liked her to give her some kind of therapy. And who would want a compliment given in that context? I was really upset. If I had been using psychology, I was blending it with my own philosophy of life, which is to tell someone if you like him or wish to compliment him--tell him, because people need to hear it and too often don't. So I answered, "No, I wasn't using psychology. I was just being

68

honest." (Pause) "I don't know enough psychology to
really use it." (Pause again--she wasn't answering me.)
"I'm sorry." I said I was sorry because I was. I really
didn't know how much I'd been playing therapist with her
and if I unconsciously had been, I was sorry, because
that's no way to be someone's friend.

We just sat there a while and she finally said that
she was done talking. I asked if I could sit there. She
said yes. I picked up a magazine and began reading. She
got up and walked away.

I really felt terrible, then--thought I'd really
blown the day, coming across as a smart aleck college kid
giving the "right answers," instead of coming across as
open, warm, and sincere. I sat there biting my finger-
nails and munching furiously on some caramels I'd brought
to share with Mary. I kept on thinking, "Oh great! Here
I am trying to help and I'm having a goddamn anxiety at-
tack!"

I just sat there like that for about ten minutes.
And then suddenly, she came back and began talking as
though nothing had happened! Maybe she believes my apol-
ogy--I hope so. Or maybe she just wanted to talk to
someone and at least I was there. Anyway, I was really
glad. I hadn't muffed things too badly, I guessed. And
that was the day.

Maybe I'm being hard on myself, demanding such sincerity and genuineness. But that's okay, because these
are qualities that I've been trying to incorporate into
my personality for a long time anyway. And I truly believe that if people dealt with each other with greater
sincerity and openness, then maybe there wouldn't be so
many people in Bethlehem.

The reasons I'm optimistic are these:

1. I feel that, somehow, Mary and I communicated--
she asked me to be sincere--and I told her I was trying;
my apology was in itself a sincere thing. It doesn't
matter that we didn't have a "smooth" day. Perhaps what
happened was better than a "smooth" day. There's something more real about people upsetting one another, as we
did, than in people making polite conversation, with no
rough spots, for an hour.

2. I learned something: treat people as equals
here; they're supposed to be "sick" and my first impulse
seems to have been "I'll say the right thing, I'll *help*
you. I'm not sick--I'll give you the right slant." Who
needs that? They are not so "crazy" that they can't see
through phoniness. In fact, they're probably sensitive
to it. Mary deserves (as well as needs) the respect in-
voked in a sincere, genuine interaction. That's what
I'll work toward.

P.S. I regret that I "goofed," but I'm human too.
If I keep on "goofing" and I'm insensitive in the future
to what I wrote about *today*, that will give me cause to
really feel bad. I'm going to see it as a mistake, one
I may make again, one that's natural, and one to watch
out for.

October 13

Today went very well. I was apprehensive when I
arrived, wondering if Mary would spend another afternoon
crying, and fearing that she perhaps might not trust me
after our last meeting, might avoid me.

But when I arrived, one of the first things she said
was that she'd been looking forward to seeing me--had even
asked the nurse if I'd called. That made me feel good and
I told her so. Also, she'd put on some make-up this time
and I commented that it looked nice. She smiled at that,
too.

The strange thing about today, though, was that it
reminded me of a play entitled "social interaction" and
we were the action. Mary was trying so *hard*! She laughed
at all my jokes (I was trying hard too!), and sometimes
the laughter seemed forced. She said all the "right"
things: for example, I mentioned that I was looking forward to graduation. She replied sweetly, "I'm sure you
are." It came too quickly, was too nice, too perfect an
answer, I thought. And she only cried once, this time.

I don't know if this is a good thing or not. She
seems to be trying to please me and to do so by "acting
normally." She's playing the game that society teaches.
Should I encourage it? Or should I try to steer our relationship toward an informal, relaxed level? I, of

course, would prefer the second. I hate games. But the second is a nonconformist type of interaction--my type-- which involves openness, directness. Society doesn't always like that. I get in trouble sometimes, for saying too much. But it's healthy for me--makes me feel free, honest. How good would it be for Mary to get used to, though? I doubt she could handle society's criticism.

Maybe I'm making too much out of this. I don't know. I'll have to see how the next meeting goes.

Oh yes, two very nice things happened toward the end: first, Mary took out an unopened package of Life- savers and offered me one. I thanked her, told her I had a great sweet tooth, and took one. We talked in group about how important it is to let the other person (the patient) give in this relationship. I'm sure if I were Mary, I'd really want to give to the person who came to see me each week, and who spent time, was friendly and pleasant, etc. I'd feel very awkward if I could not. So I think that's why she offered me the Lifesaver.

Also, she's told me she's afraid people are "fright- ened of her," won't want to meet her. When it was time to leave, Russ, the boy who I get my ride with, and Roberta, another student, came over to us to tell me it was time to leave. I introduced them to Mary. Roberta said "Hi"; Russ, who's very warm, reached out his hand to Mary with a big grin and said, "I'm pleased to meet you." He really sounded sincere. Mary looked startled, then gave him her hand and said "Hello." I think that was a nice encounter. She's probably trying to figure out why he was so friendly! Why to her!

Russ and I discussed it and sometime he's going to sit and talk a bit. It seems as though she could use that kind of experience again and again.

I realize it can't be helped but it seems insane (no pun intended) that Mary's, and any other patient's, most frequent company is other disturbed people. How can she possibly get an accurate evaluation of herself in rela- tion to others when the only models are guided by serious personal problems? To be more concrete, she was telling me that people are afraid of her, they know she's bad. I asked why she thought that. She replied that she went to a hospital dance the other night and a young girl

there was afraid to approach her, wouldn't come near. I
tried explaining that the girl was probably quite shy,
and might have been afraid of many, many people. (I really think this was the case because Mary projects a very
quiet, unhappy, unassuming image. I don't see how she
could seem threatening in and of herself.) She didn't
answer me. But she didn't disagree. I hope we can discuss it again. I added that *I* felt comfortable with her,
not afraid at all. And that there were some people who
certainly frightened me. (I added the last because I
wanted to let her know that she *could* have frightened me,
I was *not* fearless! This was in case she tried some ra-
tionalization that I was afraid of no one.)

   And that was the day.

October 20

   Not much happened today, but I'm a bit worried.
Mary was heavily drugged--she was almost falling asleep.
But when we did speak, she began complimenting me. That
was nice, but it seemed as though the entire conversation
revolved around her calling me an "angel," on how nice my
hair was, etc. It was all a bit too sweet, artificial,
superficial, for my taste.

   I'm worried because it seems as though she's viewing
me in an unrealistic light. I'm no savior, but she's
treating me like one. What if I goof? Then what will
she think? I'm certainly not going to take the role of
a "friendly local volunteer." I'm going to behave like
myself, which is a person with faults, faults she'll have
to realize, face. We'll see what happens next time.

   I realize I've never even described Mary, so I'll
tell something about her now. She's forty-three years
old, but looks about ten years older because she always
looks so depressed and tired. Also, she's had a very
hard life from what I've gathered; thus she looks even
older. She's slender, with short brown hair and a thin
face with hollow cheekbones. She's about five feet six
inches tall.

   She was married at twenty and has six children. Her
husband left her several years ago, according to Mrs.
Meredith, the social worker. Mary rarely mentions him,

and never has said she's been separated when she does mention him.

She's been to Bethlehem five times since 1956, and has been in a hospital in Westbridge and a nursing home as well.

She cries easily, and often; she gets very depressed and is convinced she's going to die, mainly because she's such a "terrible person" and deserves to. I suspect she was drugged because she's so depressed.

One positive thing that happened today was that Mary wanted to go for a walk, despite being tired from the drugs. Unfortunately, I asked the nurse, who said "No." That bothered me; I asked why and the nurse replied that Mary had been very depressed lately and might cry on the grounds. I did not see what difference it would make if she cried outside rather than inside! I thought it was a good sign to want to go out. Anyway, I asked if perhaps we could get permission to leave next Wednesday and the nurse said she'd check with the doctor.

October 27

I didn't like today. I guess I've been riding on a wave of optimism and now I've got to face the situation more realistically. What I mean is, I've been working with two premises that aren't all that valid. The first premise was that Mary really wasn't very disturbed. The second was that all she needed was someone warm and accepting (me!) and she'd open right up and begin to get well.

Oh well.

Mary has a very serious problem: she can't or won't (or both) get close to other people. And I'm not going to "cure" her! Especially in four easy sessions!

Today was quite inconsistent. It began by Mary's becoming angry with me for "asking too many questions," moved on to a change in her mood so that she spent a great deal of time complimenting me, and ended with her telling me she wanted to hear nothing about my family or friends, just wanted to pretend I came to visit her, and had no other life outside. I felt bad about asking too many questions. I explained that I'd done so because it seemed that all we ever talked about was me. Maybe I should cool it on the questions, take them a little more slowly. I wouldn't like having too many questions thrown in my face.

She remained in a rather cold mood and when I told her we now had permission to go for a walk, she said she didn't want to. I was really annoyed. She seemed to be reacting like a spoiled child. I guess she noticed my annoyance because that's when she began saddling me with more compliments about being an angel, etc. I finally told her I was flattered but a bit embarrassed because she'd complimented me so much and so extravagantly. I think that she did this because she wants me to like her, wants me to keep coming, yet is only willing to give on a superficial level like compliments. She herself seemed to try to tell me this when she later said she wanted to know me only as a visitor, not as someone real, with a life outside. She told me she "had to pretend." I told her I would not pretend with her, it was not honest or realistic. She said she was afraid to get involved, for she was "going to die" soon. I asked if she was ill. She replied, "No, it's in my head."

Perhaps the above seems like a disorganized account. That's because the conversation was disorganized! In essence, though, Mary seemed to be saying she: 1) wanted to have me keep visiting her; 2) did not want to risk the pains or dangers of an involved relationship; 3) realized she was ill and that much of what she believed was a product of her own mind.

That last seems very important. I want to bring it up in the future, if possible. As long as she can realize that much of this is in her imagination, maybe, just maybe, there's some chance. I don't want to hope too much, though. Today showed me that Mary is quite good at manipulating relationships, manipulating *me*, so that she maintains the "push-pull" interaction which might be her very problem. (She pushes me away and pulls me back.) At the end of the afternoon, she was very cheerful and gave me a quick hug, saying, "Well, now, we didn't have too bad a visit, did we?" I told her even if we had, I'd be back. She didn't always have to compliment me or feel like talking. I'd still return. I hope she believes me.

I really don't want to spend the next semester-and-a-half being called an angel!!

Next week, I'm going to wear jeans and a workshirt, in the hope that she will have nothing in my appearance to compliment. I guess that's pulling the rug out from under her feet, but if she really feels anxious, I'm sure she'll come up with another substitute for real conversation.

November 3

Today was uneventful. Actually, it was pretty good. Mary didn't compliment me once. (She couldn't; I looked terrible!) She spent most of the day gossiping about a new patient. She almost seemed like a normal person. Maybe what I said about my being unwilling to pretend, plus my returning even if she didn't compliment me, had an effect. I hope so.

November 10

Today was hectic. When I came on the ward, Mary immediately approached me and told me she "needed my help." She said she was in terrible trouble and could I please get her a lawyer. I told her if she were in legal trouble, she wouldn't be there. She said the hospital took court cases and she was one, and *please*, speak to the social worker, find out for myself about the trouble and get her a lawyer!!

I suspected it wasn't true but still, maybe she was a court case awaiting trial or something. So I went to see Mrs. Meredith, the social worker. I learned that Mary was *not* a court case and was in no trouble whatsoever, nor had she ever been.

When I returned, we had a conversation which consisted of Mary's telling me one delusion after another, and my telling her what the story really was.

The conversation began by my saying that we really had to have a talk. I'd spoken with Mrs. Meredith, who really would know, and Mary was in *absolutely no trouble* nor had she ever done anything to get her in trouble with

the law. I emphasized this idea strongly and kept repeating it and rewording it for about five minutes.

Mary looked puzzled. Then she told me she had "special powers" to hurt people. I told her that was ridiculous, that she was just a woman who had no more power to
hurt than I did. I then added that this was all in her
imagination, it was not the truth. (She had mentioned
her imagination a few weeks earlier, so I decided to
bring it up now.)

She did not disagree with me. However, she said
that it wasn't her fault that her mind was this way;
there were spacemen "twisting" her mind. I told her no,
that was her imagination speaking again. Only she could
untwist things. I grew brave and asked her to please believe me, I was telling the truth. She replied that in
her heart she wanted to but her mind kept stopping her.

I hope she thinks about our conversation. It's the
first time we ever seriously discussed what was happening
in her mind. Once more, I don't want to be too optimistic; she's been this way for at least the fifteen years
she's spent in and out of institutions and who knows how
much further back in her life the illness extends. But
while I want to keep a check on my hopes, I intend to
keep trying very, very hard.

November 17

Today I brought my guitar to the hospital. Several
patients gathered around and we all sang. Unfortunately,
I didn't know any of the songs Mary requested, and I worried that she felt left out and/or jealous of the attention I gave the others.

The problem, if it does exist, isn't too serious because I'm coming back for two hours tomorrow morning. I
intend to spend the entire time with Mary. The hospital
is holding a Christmas bazaar in the lobby and we are
going to go.

I hope she still wants to go tomorrow. It will be
the first time we've gone anywhere together. A bazaar
seemed like a good place to go because it's so bright and
exciting. Hope it works out.

November 18

Today went well, in a bumpy sort of fashion. When
I arrived, Mary was in tears. She said we couldn't go
because she had no money. She clung to me, crying. I
hugged her and smiled and said I was broke too, but we
didn't have to buy anything. She replied we still
couldn't go...she just couldn't for many reasons. So
we decided to stay on the ward.

I wanted a cup of coffee and Mary said she'd come
with me. To get to the coffee shop, we had to go to the
bazaar (my intention). Once we were there, Mary could
not tear herself away! The dresses were almost free
(twenty-five cents and fifty cents) and at my urging, she
bought two. And I really had to urge. She'd weep and
say she didn't deserve them, she was unlike other people,
etc. I told her that was untrue, of course she deserved
them, etc.

Then we had some coffee and doughnuts and returned
to the ward. Mary was anxious to try on the dresses.
When one didn't fit, she broke down again and decided to
give it away. I again argued that it had been a good
buy, that the color was good for her, and why didn't she
just take it in with a needle and thread? She finally
agreed.

We went through the same argument while she mended
the dress. Mary kept saying she was doing a terrible
job, God did not want her to have the dress, she was no
good, didn't deserve it, etc. After attempting to convince her otherwise two or three more times, I just grew
silent. She folded up the dress and put it aside. Then
she asked, "Do you think I deserve the dress?" I guess
all day she'd been asking my opinion, and now I realized
she really valued it. I answered emphatically "*Yes*!" and
then I grinned and asked her why she was taking so long
to fix the damn thing. She laughed too and resumed
sewing.

She again mentioned God's not wanting her to have
it. I remember thinking she was terrible egocentric,
even if in a negative way, so I replied that God had more
important things to worry about: wars, starvation, etc.
One woman wearing a dress was no problem. In fact, it
probably made him happy, as new dresses were nice, pleas-

ant things.

She listened carefully. I don't think she'd ever
thought of it that way.

It was a good day; a shopping trip and a snack. For
me, that was nothing. For Mary, it was a momentous event,
tied in with her *worth as an individual*. No wonder she'd
been afraid to go; treating herself to a dress meant eval-
uating whether or not she was fit to have one, whether or
not she was a decent human being. How terrifying such a
"small thing" really was to her.

Toward the day's end, when she began crying for
about the eighth time, I decided to try something new.
She seems to get "stuck" on certain ideas. I guess the
clinician would say "obsessed." Once she begins a certain thought pattern about how she's evil, has wicked
powers, and so forth, she's on a mental treadmill that
she can't seem to stop.

So I interrupted her amid her crying, saying, "Will
you do me a favor!" She stopped for a moment, asked
"What?" I asked if next time she were about to cry and
was thinking these terrible things, she would try remembering last week's conversation; that was the one in
which I reassured her over and over that she was not evil,
had no powers, etc. She said she'd try, she really wants
to have "good thoughts."

I suppose in my doing that, in making such a sugges-
tion, I went beyond the bounds of a friendship--I played
"therapist." I realize I have to watch out; I'm not
trained, I could really hurt her. Yet I can't help
feeling that at most what I've suggested will help, but
that probably it will have no effect whatsoever. It
seems as though Mary couldn't get any worse than she is
now, being at the point of not wanting to live.

Anyway, I suggested that she try really remembering;
try to remember my voice, where we were sitting, the words
I'd used, the whole scene. I hope that her attempting to
remember all this will switch her focus to more pleasant
ideas and she'll gain some way to control her mind when
it begins to wander.

November 23

Today was very depressing. Mary was about as unhappy as I've ever seen her. She hasn't worn the dresses, she talked of killing herself, and she's terrified to go home for Thanksgiving. She told me that, apparently, the doctors lessened her medication when she went home this past weekend. They thought she'd improved. (Probably because she went to the bazaar.) As a result, she could not sleep. She heard all kinds of voices, had terrible nightmares. Thus she took some of her old medication which she had at home. The doctors, of course, were furious with her. And she's afraid to go home again without medication, for fear of the nightmares, which were terrifying.

It seems as though the doctors really rushed things. I realize it's much better if a patient can get along without drugs. But this withdrawal of medication was so abrupt! What happened to the sensitive, well-thought-out care a person with such serious problems is entitled to?

And where do I fit in? Am I doing more harm than good? I did "force" her, in a sense, to behave normally. But of course, I didn't realize that the doctors would respond like this, would act so quickly, rashly. It's almost negative reinforcement for normal behavior: "Be good and we'll take away all your supports."

Maybe I'm too excited right now to be fair. Perhaps this is all a delusion of hers, perhaps she did get the medication. I should have asked the nurse. I was afraid to, though, afraid the nurse would become angry with me for "interfering." But so what? I should have found out anyway.

I'm also depressed because I suspect that despite my intellectual awareness of Mary's being very disturbed, I continue to hope for recovery. I do, I know. Especially after the bazaar and the day we dealt with her delusions. It really seemed as though we were getting somewhere. But fifteen years of thinking this way....

Maybe all I should attempt is to have a good time together. I don't know.

I was at a loss as to how to comfort her. I hadn't expected such depression.

I feel very foolish. My expectations have been (and still are, I guess) way out of proportion; the hospital staff seems more a hindrance than a help; one good day caused Mary so much anxiety and anguish that the fun hardly seems worth it. I feel foolish and helpless and very depressed.

December 3

Today Mary and I challenged hospital rules. She wasn't allowed to make a phone call home, supposedly because she cries too much when she does phone; thus the nurses don't deem her "healthy" enough to exercise that privilege.

So, at my urging, Mary and I checked the listing of "patients' rights" posted in the lobby. I was almost positive they had the right to make private phone calls, and that was true. I grew angry, as did Mary, and we decided to return and speak to the ward nurse about it. I *stressed* that we had to be nice if we wanted to get anywhere, but Mary kept muttering about what a "dirty trick" it was, and I worried that she might not keep her "cool." I guess she worried too, because she asked me to speak to the nurse for her.

While in the nurses' station, things really became tense. First, I was told that Mary couldn't make calls because she became "too emotional" over the phone and cried too much. Apparently, the hospital bends that law as it sees fit. I was trying to be very polite, to explain that Mary became even more overwrought when they wouldn't let her call, and could they please *explain* to her why she couldn't phone? She's so paranoid that she interprets this kind of thing as a sign of persecution, especially when no reason is given.

Just then, Mary walked in and asked me to come see her soon. She seemed tense, as though she wanted my conversation with the nurses to end quickly. The nurses shut the door of their office on her, saying, "In a minute, Mary." It was quite condescending, I thought, having the door closed right in front of you, especially when people were discussing *you* behind that door!

The nurses then began to tell me how much trouble
Mary is, how she and her husband can't get along because
of her behavior, etc. It seemed more like a coffee
klatch than a psychiatric nurses' station! Really catty,
and for what reason? I kept thinking the nurses were
trying to get me to "side" with them, and their tactic
was to prove to me how incompetent and crazy Mary was!
Just then, Mary flung open the door and said, "Secrets
again!" She then slammed it and stormed off down the
hall. I thought, "Right on, Mary!" but ran out after
her. I suddenly was afraid she'd think I was "against
her" also. She did. She began accusing me of spying on
her, etc., etc., and stormed away from me each time I
tried to talk to her. One patient screamed at me, "Ya
got no right coming here, snooping!"

What a mess. I was speechless, and was torn between
screaming back, "*No*, you're all wrong!" or running out of
the ward. To make things worse, the nurses kept winking
at me! Mary had "proved" they were right--or I guess
that's what they thought.

Anyway, what I did do was approach Mary one last
time and say, "Look, I know you won't talk, but I want
you to know that I don't think this is any way for
friends to work out a problem." She didn't answer, so
I walked away. I felt really preachy saying it, but it
was either say something calmly and constructively or
scream, "Jesus Christ, Mary, you're driving me crazy!
Don't you even know who your friends are?" I didn't want
to scream. It was our "first fight" and I thought I
should be "patient" or some such thing. I suspect we'll
have run-ins in the future and then I'll lose my temper
more freely!

Mary apologized to me about ten minutes later. We
had coffee and I stressed that she had to "play the
game," i.e., control herself somewhat, in order to "get
privileges." I also emphasized that it *was* a game, that
she had every right to make that telephone call; we were
helpless but that didn't mean we were in the wrong.

I'm utterly exhausted. I feel as though I ran the
gamut of emotions today, from anger at the rules and
nurses, to hurt at Mary's personal accusations, to pride

at Mary's telling off the nurses. Right now, I'm feeling
unsettled and depressed. The rules seem inflexible and
the nurses seem petty. I don't want to be at odds with
the hospital staff! I can see why some patients are too
irrational to use the phone and, much as I hate to admit
it, I've been taught to respect authority--blind author-
ity--and the idea of bucking it shakes me--scares me--
even though I think they're wrong in Mary's case. Even
if she does seem too disturbed to phone, at least they
should tell her that; she was only told she didn't have
permission. And what kind of effect does that have?
1) Her paranoia is reinforced; 2) she is not given the
chance to "learn" what behavior will make life there (and
perhaps elsewhere in society) run more smoothly.

About the only *good* thing that happened was Mary's
anger at the nurses. She still has some pride and refused to be stepped on with gossip. I told her that it
was "normal" to lose her temper at such things and that
I was glad she had, but she should be more careful because she could get in trouble for it, not necessarily
because she was wrong, however.

Nevertheless, it was a nerve-racking, frustrating
day. I'm glad it's over.

December 10

Today was quite calm, compared to last time. Mary
did not seem to want to discuss what had happened, which
bothered me; I thought we might be closer after such a
"fiasco." Maybe she did too, so she was cool and taci-
turn.

One nice thing did happen: I played some Christmas
carols on the organ and Mary sang. Her mood became much
warmer once we discussed Christmas. We even walked
around the building to see the decorations.

I'm going to see if I can hunt up some Christmas
decorations for her room. It's really stark. All the
stuff for Christmas is in the lobby or corridors and
maybe Christmas things in her room would cheer her up.
I'm latching on to that holiday--anything to liven up
Mary and get her mind off her self-hatred. When she
talks about Christmas, she becomes quite likable, so I

have a stake in it too!!

December 17

Today I brought decorations and a small Christmas tree. I was told the tree had to go because it was real. Only nonflammable ones are allowed. Fire hazard, etc. What can I say? I see the point but--it smelled so great and it would have been so *uninstitutional--so much like past Christmases* at *home*.

Someone in lecture said that institutions like Bethlehem cannot be improved. The whole system is based on custodial care and the only answer is a new system, like halfway houses. I'm beginning to understand and agree. Such a *big* place has to have those rules to avoid chaos. Any large institution dedicated to protecting people's safety--hospitals, jails, reformatories--must have organization, rules, to keep running. But human beings cannot always be slaves to routine and rules. They have to have an escape, and for most people the escape is home, even if it's only a dormitory room--it's your own, private place. Mary can't escape to any place. No wonder she hates it there.

Anyway, we made a doll out of some of the decorating material I'd brought, plus used the other decorating material on the ward tree. But it wasn't much fun. Mary was in a bad mood and insisted that the tree needed no more decorations. She put a damper on my enthusiasm and on the other patients' as well. It is almost as though she *wanted* to be unhappy. I grew angry and told her I was going to decorate whether she liked it or not; I'm Jewish and haven't done many Christmas trees and I wanted to have some fun!!! She told me I was making her so nervous that she'd put out her cigarette. I told her she put it out herself and stormed away. As always, she apologized later and we "forgot" about it.

I'm glad it happened. She seems convinced that not only is she one of the world's most evil people but she's also "special" in that she expects her every mood to control my behavior. For instance, she begins to cry and constantly expects my sympathy even though her "problem" is usually in her imagination, and she will admit that when we talk. I told her that I can only "sympathize" about things that are real and she *immediately* stopped crying when I said so. In the same sense, she attempts to control my behavior by being sulky when I'm happy.

I guess what it boils down to is this: Mary likes to play games. There's the "I've got troubles, comfort me" game. That gets affection, plus being a neat way to avoid honest interaction, since the only troubles she tells me are fictitious. Then there's the "I'm in a bad mood so I won't participate" game. That also brings attention and is a neat escape from participation in a threatening activity.

I don't like being manipulated. And I don't like things always revolving around *her*. It's a weird kind of egotism, having all things center around you because you're so messed up.

At any rate, I'm not going to play and today I told her, in so many words. I feel so hard and cruel, yet I can't see how going along with her irrational behavior will do any good. I guess sometimes honesty has to be cruel.

December 23

I sent Mary a letter over this vacation, plus a very religious Christmas card, because she's devoutly religious. (She'd told me she wanted no present.) I tried to be warm and friendly in the letter. I hope she liked it.

January 3

Today brought good news. Mary is on the open ward and suddenly seems much improved. We had a *good* talk about how she might bring mending from home to the hospital, since she's bored. She never showed an interest in doing something before!

I also told her that being on this ward was a good sign--it meant you were closer to going home. She said she hadn't even known that.

She looked much calmer and I told her so as well as complimenting her on her appearance. I wish I could compliment her more often, but she so seldom looks good or does anything that I have little material to compliment her on! I'd like to build her confidence, and now that she's bored, maybe I have a chance. Next week I'm bringing a flower-making kit. It's easy to do and I'm sure she'll feel a sense of accomplishment when she makes them.

Our friendship, though still not as open verbally as I'd like, has progressed in other ways. Today, Mary *asked* me for a hug!!! I've hugged her before and we often stroll with our arms linked. But she's never been so free in searching out affection. I guess she's sure that she'll get it, and I'm glad. Naturally, I hugged her. Then, so as not to make it seem as though she was always the "poor, needy" one, I asked if I could have a hug, too. She seemed surprised, and gave me a big hug.

It was a nice day. Again, I'm hesitantly hopeful.

January 17

Today was the nicest one we've ever had. Not only did Mary make the flowers, she urged two other patients to participate and helped me teach them. Later we had coffee and had a great time gossiping about some obnoxious male patient who tried to pick me up!! The whole day just seemed so much like the things I'd do with a friend. Even though I'm twenty-one and Mary is forty-three, she acts as though she were my age (or perhaps younger, at times). We made something together, then enjoyed some jokes about my near pickup. I really liked her today and told her what a good time I had.

Later Mary began to mutter about being no good. This time, I could point out how kind she'd been to those two patients, how most people weren't that nice. She thought a moment and then smiled--even laughed--and agreed! I also told her she'd done a better job on the flowers than had the other women, and we discussed how her teenage daughters would like them, how Mary could teach them. I could see she was feeling good.

Mary says she's going to ask her husband to sign her out. We talked about how she's afraid of the future. I tried to tell her that there could be joy as well as sorrow, but she kept saying she wanted to live in another world without pain. Though I managed to direct the talk so that she conceded there was only this world with its joy as well as pain, I'm still worried. I don't think they'll let her go home, and if they do, I don't think she'll make it very long.

I tried to tell her she might not go, but she didn't want to discuss the possibility. I foresee a big disappointment and dread seeing her next time. I'm sure she'll be in bad shape after not being able to go home.

January 27

Well, she's on the closed ward again, and refused to tell me what happened. Again, she was cold. I found myself returning her coldness. I couldn't help it. I get so tired of always having to get things going. Is that wrong? If I'm to treat her as an equal, shouldn't I expect her to pull her load of the friendship?

Later we had another discussion about how she hated herself, had caused a world disaster, and so forth. I just couldn't take it. I was about to take her hand and comfort her but I stopped short, saying it wasn't real, so I couldn't be upset for her. I asked how she could expect me to discuss a tragedy that had never occurred. She didn't answer. She looked pretty surprised that I had said it, though, and immediately dropped the subject.

I don't know if I did that for her own good or because I was angry at her self-centeredness. Whatever, I feel both guilty and relieved: guilty because I denied her the affection she wanted, and relieved because I could feel anger instead of pity. Somehow I see her as more powerful--more my equal--when I can grow angry than when I can feel sorry for her.

My feelings are so mixed. She wants love, and that touches me. But she reaches out for it in such a twisted manner, "Love me, I'm so pitiful," that I react with anger at the dishonesty, the manipulation. I become even more resentful when after one of our few real, honest talks, she becomes cold and hard. She's screwing the whole relationship up and driving *me* crazy!!!

February 4

Today I brought my electric rollers and set Mary's
hair. But the afternoon wasn't too pleasant. She was to
go home for the weekend but at the last minute, she lost
"permission" and had to remain at the hospital. That was
because she'd been talking about slashing her wrists and
was reported; thus the staff thought it was dangerous to
let her go.

Mary told me she never meant to do it and that it
was a "dirty trick" to keep her there. I tried over and
over to explain to her that she had to be careful--that
she was *responsible* for her actions and that what she
said was *important*--she had to think before she spoke.

She cried and refused to agree or answer.

I also told her my patience was running short.

I feel that I'm failing, somehow. I know that I'm
only reacting normally, yet I blame myself for becoming
angry. I'm afraid if this happens again, if Mary gets
herself in a jam and then blames others or looks for sympathy when she doesn't deserve it, that I'll really blow
my stack. Perhaps that would be the best thing for her.
Maybe if I come right out and tell her I consider her an
adult--that she has to face up to life--she'll try harder.
Right now, the only thing that's expected of her is that
she act crazy or stay out of the way, both of which she
does quite well. I suppose my guilt feelings arise from
the standard conception I always had of the "mentally
ill": "poor, frightened people in need of acceptance and
love." All that may be true but it isn't the whole story.
One could add this sentence to the description: "In need
of love--but so afraid of hurt and failure that many play
intricate games; games that get attention for a while,
but eventually bring on anger and resentment, thus bringing on the very isolation feared. Games that manipulate
people by pulling them forth, then pushing them away."

February 8

In discussion, someone suggested that I give Mary
affection *before* she breaks down and cries, laments, etc.
It seemed so obvious when it was said that I was really

angry with myself for not realizing that I should have
been doing it. Now that I think about it, I see that she
must be starved for affection, both physical and verbal,
since she has no friends there and only sees her family
on weekends! I feel really dense. I've been warm and
affectionate but never really made a point of noticing
her need. I was more concerned with getting onto an honest, open level. What a fool! I know I can't function
without emotional support and though I've given her a
lot, I still feel I have not given *enough*. (That doesn't
mean I'm going to play her games, though.) Next time
I'll begin looking more toward her need for affection and
trying to fulfill some of it.

I'm writing about "today" in retrospect. I think
Mary knew I was growing impatient and consequently, she
was pleasant and reserved. The day was uneventful, with
the exception of one incident: a young high school student who was a volunteer mistook me for a patient; I decided to "play along," to see, even for an instant, how
she'd treat me and how I'd feel. The conversation lasted
approximately five minutes and I felt as though she was
talking down to me, treating me as though I was not only
"dangerous" but simple. And my greatest desire was to
shock her! A small sample of what being a patient must
feel like! The girl was sickly sweet, never stopped
smiling, and stuck to "safe" questions, such as "do you
have any hobbies?" Every answer I gave brought an immediate compliment: my name was nice, my hobbies were
nice, bet I was good at them, etc. At no time did I feel
as though she regarded me as an individual. I could have
been any "patient" and received that bland, guarded, in-
sincere approach. I found that I quickly stopped smiling,
began answering in monosyllables, and barely avoided being
rude. I really think that if she'd stayed on five more
minutes I'd have told her my hobby was strangling babies;
I would have loved to have seen her face!

Mary thought it was really funny. I later asked her
if many volunteers were like that. She said "yes" and
that she didn't like them. I wonder how long it takes
before that approach stops being a joke and really begins
affecting one's self-concept.

February 15

Today was different. In retrospect, I realize it
was not only a turning point in our relationship, it was
the beginning of my *really* believing Mary is a competent
human being and believing it enough to tell her so, not
as a comforting phrase but as revelation of the obvious.

"Institutionalization reinforces dependent behavior."
I've heard that statement ever since I took my first sociology course, but its true meaning came through to me
just in the past few weeks. When an individual enters a
mental hospital, he probably has no faith in himself as a
competent being. Being hospitalized--a way of saying,
"You failed out there"--reinforces that lack of faith.
And the institutional routine whereby one's needs are totally taken care of by staff, including cooking, laundry,
etc., serves as a final daily reminder that one is not in
charge of his own life. It seems that even the most
self-sufficient person would begin to doubt himself.
Furthermore, he would assume a dependent role, once he
learned that "privileges" hinge upon staying out of the
way, not causing extra work for the attendants. Yet often, learning a skill, like sewing, or cooking, requires
"a mess," losing one's temper at failure, noise, disar-
ray, confusion. O.k., "institutionalization reinforces
dependence."

The privilege system and rules imply that the patient, unlike the staff, is a different type of person,
one whose behavior is unpredictable and possibly dangerous. All of that really affected my view of Mary. I remember the first few times I lit a cigarette for her. I
kept holding the matches in my hand for fear she might
set herself on fire!

Until I learned to trust her, I was impressed enough
by the authority of the hospital to believe Mary was incapable of maintaining rational behavior even for our
short hour together. Why would the nurse always warn me
to be careful when borrowing a stapler? Something must
be wrong with Mary if such precautions were being taken!
I am not denying that many patients are committed to a
hospital like Bethlehem State because they are believed

dangerous to themselves or others. However, the effect
of constant surveillance over a person's everyday activities certainly could deepen both a patient's self-doubt
and a visitor's mistrust of that patient so that even
when danger no longer existed, the image of the patient
as unreliable would live on.

It seems that a majority of the changes need to be
made in the patients' *environment*, not in their personalities. How much good am I doing telling Mary she can
make it when so many rules around her suggest that she
can't?

Self-fulfilling prophecy, etc., etc. Somebody has
to step in and break the "vicious circle." At best, that
circle should be broken by altering the damaging agent,
the institution. The only alternative is to alter its
message by offering Mary a competing one. Which is what
I did today.

When Mary began her lament--"Wait'll the newspapers
print what I've done," "I'm useless, no good"--I lost my
temper, really let go, for the first time. I told her I
was sick and tired of all this, it wasn't true and we
both knew it. I said I felt she was blaming herself
needlessly and almost seemed to want to hurt herself.
She could be quite useful if she spent less time crying
and more time doing things like bringing mending from
home, going to OT, taking patients for walks who could go
only with another person. I countered her every objec-
tion to her competence. I pointed out that it was she
who had drawn out some patients who wanted to make flowers with us but who I failed to draw out myself. It was
she who hemmed the dresses purchased at the bazaar, and
did them quickly and well. I brought up every good quality of hers that I could think of. She finally answered
that I was a lot of talk--or, "prove it some more"--so I
said it was *she* who was a lot of talk but I'd be just as
bad if I agreed with her self-criticisms. I then re-
counted more of her good traits--how she could be so
friendly to me, how much she seemed to worry and care
about her children--until I was exhausted. She seemed to
listen to every word. My "speech" held little sympathy
or gentleness. It was more the words of an equal saying,
"Damn it, stop pitying and blaming yourself. You're a
complete human being, now start living like one!"

Getting rid of emotional problems like Mary's is a major task in itself. But doing so by bucking her very environment seems enormous to me. I don't know how she can make it, in that setting. Perhaps if she were in a halfway house, where she had her autonomy and some responsibility, it would be better. I don't know. But I think I'll continue to tell her these things. I really do believe she's capable of far more than she's doing.

March 12

Today was rather uneventful. I've been out for a few weeks with a bad back, which has placed me in a bad mood since I might need surgery. So it was difficult for me to have much enthusiasm or energy when visiting Mary.

I really wish she'd pull her weight of the friendship. Simply because I wasn't in the best of moods didn't mean we needed to have a dull day. Why couldn't she carry the responsibility for our enjoying the day? Oh well.

March 19

Today was really depressing and disappointing. I'm going to have to return home for about a month's bed rest due to my back trouble. That means dropping courses, not graduating in June, and worrying about the possibility of complicated surgery if the bed rest doesn't work.

I wasn't in the mood to give much of anything emotionally, and I guess I shouldn't have gone because today was terrible. When I arrived at the hospital, Mary was in a poor mood. I explained to her about my leaving and told her I was sorry I wouldn't be able to visit her any more. She was really formal in her reaction. She almost sounded like a school teacher as she frozenly said, "Well, Ellen, I'll miss you." I suppose she was hurt that I was leaving her and she was having trouble offering even those words. But I wanted more--I didn't want her to "*understand*"--I wanted to hear she was sorry about my trouble, that she cared, that it was really too bad. I guess I wanted her to give me some understanding, as I had been trying to give her all these months. If she could not or would not reciprocate the giving, then our whole friendship seems a sham to me.

Anyway, I tried telling her how upset I was about my back, how it hurt and I was frightened, but she really avoided conversation. She wouldn't give an inch. I found my defenses going up--I felt really hurt, hostile and put out. The rest of the afternoon, I was a combination of insensitivity and honesty; when she again began her lament about wanting to die, I didn't respond kindly or tactfully. I simply snapped that she took things too damn seriously (her reason for wanting to die was the fact that we couldn't get the stereo to work). I also told her that she simply had to take things one at a time and stop interpreting every imperfection as a crisis. But I didn't say these things gently. My tone was one of anger, annoyance. I was fed up.

She challenged me--said I was "full of soup"--I told her she was full of soup. She then snapped, "I wanna die. What's wrong with that?" I remember thinking she seemed to enjoy the morbidity of the thought. I answered that there was nothing wrong with it, it was just a waste of what could be a good thing if she tried. The conversation was an argument really. We were both angry: I at her self-centeredness, she at my lack of sympathy.

When it was time to leave, I began the good-byes. I figured that despite our bitter afternoon we had some sort of friendship--so I started to tell her to take care but before I could finish, she snapped "good-bye" and walked off.

I felt hurt for a second, then really, really angry. Who the hell did she think she was? I don't care how many problems she has, I'm human too, and I tried to share some love with her--and when it was time to go, because I was sick, she'd packed up her feelings and left me standing in the middle of my sentence! I know I must have hurt her, but damn it, one can't always think of the "poor mental patient's" feelings!

Actually, I had expected Mary to act like a normal, mature adult. I had expected her to give instead of take. And she didn't want to play the part. I'm angry and hurt, but I realize that for me, what happened was a good thing--that's because it shows I've come to see Mary as an equal, thus I expected her to behave like one. I want to throw away all the garbage I've grown up with, garbage that led me to see the mental patient as a pitiful creature of whom we should expect nothing good.   I want to throw it away but it won't mean much unless mental institutions throw away the incompetency idea too. Then, maybe it won't be as easy for someone like Mary to avoid life.   Then, maybe, her problems can be worked upon rather than increased.

April 15

Well, my back is o.k. and today I returned to see Mary.   I admit I didn't want to go, after our last visit. I was afraid she'd be cold and I'd feel hostile.   In fact the only reason I did go was my academic commitment.

Surprisingly, we had a good time.   We sat outside because it was a beautiful day.   The afternoon was uneventful--we made pleasant conversation and decided upon a picnic for next week.   It was as though nothing had ever gone wrong.

April 22

The picnic went well too.   I've never seen Mary behave so "normally."   There's really nothing to record because it was a pleasant and uneventful day.

April 24

Today was a terrible switch.   The class took a group of patients out to campus.   Mary couldn't come because she hasn't got her family's permission to leave the grounds.

When we brought the patients back to the ward, I went over to say hello to Mary.   The first words out of her mouth were, "What's the matter--don't I rate?"   For a moment I didn't know what she meant.   Then it hit me that she was upset about not being able to come to campus. I tried to explain but she wouldn't listen.   Finally, she told me to never come see her again and walked away.

I realize now she must have felt rejected and hurt. I'll still come to see her next week. I hope we can discuss it.

I'm getting tired. It's really a drain to be with a person whose feelings are so sensitive, who reads rejection into situations so easily. It's hard to keep trying to give and to understand.

May 1

Oh boy! Today Mary firmly insisted that I never return. I think she was still upset about missing the outing, plus the fact that I spoke with another patient for a time today; that may have made her jealous.

I tried very hard to talk about her anger but all she would do was say she didn't want to argue and would I please leave.

I spoke with Mrs. Meredith, the social worker, for a good hour afterwards. She sees the anger and hurt on Mary's part as a good sign, a sign that Mary cares! She definitely thinks I should return to show I care. I don't want to. I'm disgusted and hurt. And I'm sick of always giving and not getting. What a mess. I don't know what to do. I told Mary she'd hurt me. She just muttered, "Too bad."

May 7

Well, I went back. I decided that Mary probably did care and if I left when she told me to, she could interpret that as a lack of caring on my part. That would probably make her feel really worthless--after nine months of visiting, I left simply because she told me to in a fit of anger. I must have been anxious to go!

I also returned because I felt that my own defenses were getting in the way of the relationship. I'd begun returning Mary's coldness with coldness of my own. That's a natural defense. But I guess someone has to give if we're to break down walls, to be trite, and since I was the one pursuing a good relationship, it might help to add some patience and compassion to my attitude.

Anyway, when I showed up she looked very surprised to see me. I told her I'd come because I wanted to see her once more before school ended and that I wanted her to know I really hoped things would get better for her. At first she didn't want to talk--said we had nothing to discuss--but then she decided to have a Coke with me. Things went very well. I told her I wouldn't have returned if I hadn't cared which is the truth. As the afternoon went on, she became really responsive and friendly. I think it meant a lot to her that I came back. Maybe she really had been testing to see if I cared.

She apologized for the last session. I said it was okay, the hospital could put anyone in a bad mood. She perked up at that and we got into a really good talk about how she felt there was no one there to talk to, how no one seemed to understand. It suddenly seemed quite logical to me when she added that all the staff was against her. It's an easy step from thinking that people are insensitive toward you to thinking they don't like you and are against you. This was the first time I'd tried to see things her way instead of trying to make her see mine. I told her what I thought--that she had reached a logical conclusion that I probably would have reached also--but that the problem lay in the staff's busyness and insensitivity, not in any real plan to hurt her. She really seemed to listen.

Then she began an intricate description of her hallucinations. I couldn't believe it. She told me about the spacemen who were controlling her mind, told me exactly what they looked like. I told her I thought everyone needed a reason to explain his or her problems and that I thought spacemen were hers. But I added I thought she was mistaken--and also, since the spacemen were invisible to all but herself, they were a poor reason, because who can catch and stop invisible spacemen?

She snapped that I must want her to blame herself. I replied that blame wasn't the word and furthermore, she wasn't the entire reason. I said I thought the hospital was the worst place for someone who was troubled. It was too cold and impersonal to cheer anyone up. Also, if someone has a hard life, that hurts too. And finally, one's mind is difficult to control. Only she could do it but it was a hard job and she shouldn't blame herself for having trouble.

She laughed nervously and blurted out that this was a strange thing to discuss, wasn't it? It was almost as though her "normal" side was objectively viewing the craziness. I replied I was glad we were talking about it--we should. She added defensively that she wasn't scared. I'm sure she was. Her knuckles were white from clenching her fists so hard.

I'm going back one last time next week. I honestly wish I were returning for nine more months. There's so much I still need to learn and so much more sensitivity that I have to develop. Most important, our friendship deepened this last visit. I honestly felt Mary had put some real trust in me, perhaps for the first time.

JP - Do you have any general impressions of the student program?

> It's nice for the patients to go out on walks and be treated to coffee. Most of the time it was Dutch treat though.

JP - Do you remember the student you had?

> Oh, yes, Ellen. I don't remember her last name though. She would try to get my mind interested in things, but I would try to shrug it off. I didn't accept her right. She was very personal and knew the predicament I was in. I didn't trust her wholly. (Pause) She bought lunch for me one day and also a carton of cigarettes. That was at the end of the year. Was for my birthday, I think.

JP - Why didn't you trust Ellen?

> That's one of my problems. I wanted to talk openly about it but she didn't want to. (Pause) I suppose that if we did, it wouldn't have helped anyway. (Sadly)

JP - What kind of girl was she?

> A Jewish-Russian girl. I thought of her as an angel. I called her my "guardian angel." I was very depressed at the time and didn't have anyone else to turn to.

JP - Did she help you?

> Yes, I feel she helped me with my confidence some. She tried to get me off my problems, but I knew I had to face them. I'm facing them better now.

JP - Yes? In what way?

Trusting people. Depending on people.
Trying to be myself.

JP - What has caused you to start to trust
people?

Don't know what to say to that one.

JP - Ever hear from Ellen since she left?

No. She gave me her address and I
could have written to her. (Pause)
She wasn't getting anywhere with me,
so she looked toward others. One time
there was a thing in the auditorium
and she didn't invite me. She also
used to talk with other patients.
(Pause) I also didn't like the way
that they live at the college. Men
and women on the same floor without
locked doors.
Also, one time there was a bazaar and
I won a necklace. I don't like jewelry
and I gave it to Ellen. I thought she
would like it. She seemed delighted
but then she said it would be worth
money later on. I felt hurt. I thought
she would keep it herself, as something
I had given her, not think of selling
it.

JP - Did you let her know you were annoyed about
that?

No, I just tossed it aside.

JP - Is that a problem you have? Very sensitive,
but don't let other people know you are annoyed?

How do you know?

JP - From what you just told me. I am a psychiatrist. (Laughing)

Am I odd?

JP - No. It's just that I guess you have the
same kinds of problems with other people
that you had with Ellen.

I trust my neighbor though.

JP - How come?

> Because she is aware of God's love and
> what it can do for us. (Pause) I'm
> just afraid I might break her heart.
> She's very kindhearted. We give her
> some milk from our farm and in return
> she gives us clothes from her shop and
> many other things.

JP - Why are you afraid of breaking your neighbor's heart?

> Well, she's a Christian Scientist and
> I'm not. I want to be a child of God
> though. I'm a real disappointment to
> myself. (Very sadly) I don't want to
> talk about it. I hear voices. They
> tell me things that are not nice.
> There is something mechanically wrong
> with my head. It's not my fault. Or
> don't you believe me? (Crying)

JP - Did Ellen believe you?

> She tried to sidetrack me.

JP - How do you know that?

> I don't want to talk about it anymore.

JP - Why don't you relax for a moment. I've got
to catch up on my notes anyhow. I do have
some other things I'd like to ask about,
o.k.?

> Yes.

JP - Do you have a student this year?

> No. I've been out of the hospital and
> supposed to go home again soon.

JP - Is it lonely here?

> Well, facing my problems I am alone.
> But I do have a friend in the hospital.
> Another patient.

JP - How come you couldn't share your problems

with Ellen?

> I got disappointed when Ellen would
> change the subject when I tried to talk
> about some of my problems.

JP - What are some of these problems?

> If you don't know, then I don't know.
> (Smiling)

JP - Can people read other people's minds?

> Well, if you can't, I'm glad.

JP - From your reluctance to share your problems,
I have a hunch that it is something you are
ashamed of?

> Yes, I told you I hear voices. (An-
> noyed) What the voices say could be
> anything. (Crying)

JP - Even dirty words?

> Yes. Why did this have to happen to me?
> I can't talk to someone who shrugs it
> off! I talked with other students, not
> Ellen, sometimes. They listened to me.
> Ellen would say, "We don't want to think
> about that." (Pause) It only leaves me
> brokenhearted after I talk about it any-
> how. (Pause) I wonder what you are
> going to do with this? (The notetaking)
> I sound like a negative person, don't I?

JP - You worry a lot, don't you? I'm just trying
to evaluate and improve the student program
and this interview is important enough to
share with others concerned with student
programs.

> I'm a real worrywart. Ellen noticed
> that. (Pause) She would bring records
> sometimes, expensive ones. New ones
> like they play on the campus. Music
> that is not even on the radio yet.

JP - Yes, styles change. (Pause) Would you have
wanted to have the relationship with Ellen,
now that you know how it went?

Let's put it this way. I wish I never
had to be in this place and never had
to have Ellen. How does that sound?

JP - O.k. But I don't believe you really answered my question.

Lots of times she was pleasant to be
with. But when she was gone the troubles were still there. (Pause) But
like my husband says, I have to learn
to think positively.

JP - Were you sorry to see Ellen leave?

Well, she was somebody to pass the time
with. I guess I was sad.

JP - That's in part why you talk with me too,
huh?

It breaks up the monotony.

JP - Do you think Ellen learned anything from
you?

She learned I'm stubborn. That I want
to trust people but I can't.

JP - What else?

That's all.

JP - Did she learn you are sensitive?

Yes.

JP - Did she learn why you stay in the hospital?

I'd rather spend my time home. I did
leave the hospital in December and I
just got back. I didn't have the prop-
er medicine. I ran out of medicine and
needed another prescription. Also, my
husband really doesn't make enough
money to buy the pills. So, I didn't
take enough medicine and then got upset.

JP - What did you learn about Ellen?

The fellow who made Ellen's breakfast
was a good cook? (Coughing) She had a
boyfriend, you know.

JP - What did you like best about Ellen?

> The way she would eat. She said she
> was always hungry. She had a good ap-
> petite but I don't.

JP - Do you think Ellen will ever become a patient?

> No! She has confidence in herself. A
> way with herself and others. She's been
> brought up in a family that loves her.
> She has enough money to go to college
> and has freedom in the college.

JP - Would you like to have a daughter like
Ellen?

> I don't like to be put on the spot like
> that. (Pause) No. She's too forward.
> Also a bit hasty and impulsive.

JP - You think that will get her into trouble in
life?

> Kids today are different. She has
> freedom, trust in God, and a mother and
> father who love her. Friends, too. No.
> She won't end up as a patient.

JP - Any similarity between her and you when you
were a girl her age?

> You must remember I got married when I
> was sixteen years old. It was a mis-
> take to get married that young.

JP - Did you talk practically like this with
Ellen?

> No. (Laughing) Most of the time, no.

JP - Dodged around, huh?

> Yes. (Pause) She played the piano for
> me. (Pause) I still think this is
> damaging. Aren't we done?

JP - No.

> I like to face the truth, but she'd
> shrug it off.

JP - Did you ever worry about upsetting her?

> A little. (Pause) I'm sorry I didn't give all my feelings to her. At the end I would have hugged and kissed her.

JP - Why didn't you?

> I felt I'd upset her if I did.

JP - You didn't want her to feel bad about leaving?

> The way she talked to me. She was like a guardian angel. She came to see me with her pants patched here and there. I'd never walk out the door like that. She'd say, "I wear them until the material is comfortable to be in." I also had to laugh about her handbag. She carried almost everything imaginable inside it.

JP - Sounds like you got to know her?

> Yes.

JP - Did she get to know you?

> Some. I really wouldn't let her. (Pause) You know, though, the university program took a lot of people out of their shell. It's pretty lonely here.

JP - I guess it is. Maybe this is a good place to stop. Thanks for answering my questions.

3

THE VOICES OF
BOYS AND GIRLS

Carol and Jane

"Where do the retarded go when they are not capable of independence, but there is no one to take care of them?" This was the question on Carol's mind as she came to know Jane during her year's visits to Bethlehem State.

In contrast to Amy, who questioned the meaning of abnormality and the reasons for Ann's hospitalization, and in contrast to Ellen, who had high aspirations for Mary and hoped to help her change, Carol quickly accepted Jane's mental retardation as an illness. She became very close to Jane, and had to learn how to cope with her own feelings of disappointment and frustration as she recognized the relationship's limitations and Jane's poor future prospects.

Even though Carol was told that Jane was "obviously mentally retarded," most retardation is really no more or no less obvious than emotional disorder. We tend to assume that mental retardation is organic, but although most severe forms, such as Down's Syndrome, stem from physical disorders of the brain, these account for only about 20 percent of persons diagnosed as mentally retarded. The remaining 80 percent, often called cultural-familial retardates, appear to be very much like most other persons except that their intellectual development is slower and this usually becomes more noticeable at school. For years the presumed cause of this major category of retardation has been inheritance of low intelli-

gence, yet recent studies show a strong relationship between the incidence of mental retardation and adverse
social, economic, and cultural status of the family.

So the same things that puzzled Amy and Ellen in the
preceding two chapters apply here too. Is Jane different
from other people? Why should she be in Bethlehem State
Hospital? How should one treat her and what should be
expected of her?

One day, Carol told the weekly support group about
being in a bus terminal in a large city and seeing a man
who was talking to himself. It turned out that he was
trying to find his way to the state hospital at Bethlehem.
His questions brought hurried replies from passers-by.
When he asked the bus driver at every stop if he was at
Bethlehem, many passengers stared and snickered. Carol
compared him to a man in her small hometown who, like
Jane, seemed both retarded and emotionally disturbed but
was helped and supported by the residents. People hired
him for odd jobs, bus drivers made sure he got off at the
right stop, and the police drove him home when it rained.
Granting that some people can't live independently, Carol
asked what makes it so difficult for them to live in our
society without a sheltering institutional environment?

In the following chapter, the reader meets Jane at
Bethlehem State Hospital, which is maintained for the
treatment of mental illness, not for the care of the retarded, and later in a privately run rest home designed
for convalescence and care of the aged. Carol, talking
about Jane in the weekly support group, said, "Bethlehem,
ironically, is the place where she is best able to maintain the greatest measure of freedom, independence, and
human dignity." She felt that the impersonal condescen-
sion of hospital staff and volunteers was easier for Jane
to live with and ignore than doting parents, brothers,
and sisters. Do you agree?

BETHLEHEM STATE HOSPITAL

MEDICAL RECORD

Jane Frank   Patient #72645

ADMISSION NOTE - JANUARY 29, 1970

This twenty-six-year-old female patient, accompanied by her father and her sister, was admitted on Temporary Care. According to the legal paper, "Patient is known to be retarded moderately, but this winter has experienced psychotic disorganization manifested by fantasy formation, converting night into day, threats to burn the house down, etc. Family has found her increasingly difficult to manage. Teeth and personal hygiene need attention. Patient is lonely. She is at times seclusive and out of contact."

On admission, the patient's intellectual capacity and functioning are very limited. She says she reached only the first grade and attended special lessons once. She was not able to do simple addition or multiplication. She looks very timid and shy. Due to patient's apparent mental retardation, it is quite difficult to assert if there are any psychotic manifestations. Medication given - Mellaril. Tentative diagnosis: Mental Retardation.

FEBRUARY 5, 1970   This retarded female patient was at first very withdrawn and secluded; later on, however, she became extremely restless, overactive, and noisy on the ward, hollering for no apparent reason. Therefore, her medication had to be changed to Thorazine. Whether or not the patient is deluded or hallucinated cannot be determined as there is extremely poor contact with her. She is also whispering to herself.

FEBRUARY 18, 1970   Following Thorazine medication, the patient became quite manageable. Presently she is friendly and talks, although

106

her conversation is very primitive and simple.
She is not noisy, she tries to keep herself
clean, and participates in OT. Her intellectual
capacity and functioning are very low. When
seen by this examiner recently, she was able to
describe all the household work that she was doing when at home. There is no evidence of delusions or hallucinations.

OCTOBER 28, 1970   ANNUAL NOTE   This twenty-six-
year-old, single female was previously admitted
January 29, 1970. She was given the diagnosis
of Moderate Mental Retardation.

FEBRUARY 24, 1971   Visit: Condition - Improved.
Care of mother. Mentally Retarded: Recovered
from psychotic episode. Will be followed-up in
out-patient clinic. After three months, she
will be discharged for good. Medication of
Thorazine given.

MARCH 15, 1971   Returned from visit by mother,
who stated that patient has not been doing well
since release from hospital. She has been hallucinating and complaining of back pains. At
times she has been noted to jerk backward and
her eyes roll upward. Patient is depressed,
disoriented as to place, but oriented to time
and person. Patient signed Voluntary Admission
form.

JUNE 17, 1971   Transferred. Patient is doing
much better. She is taking care of herself and
her hygiene is good. She has ground privileges
and may now be tried on an open ward.

JUNE 28, 1971   Transferred. Patient seems to
be responding to hallucinations, talks to herself aloud. At times agitated. She is in need
of closer supervision.

JULY 14, 1971   ANNUAL NOTE   This twenty-seven-
year-old, single female's last admission was
January 29, 1971. She was given the diagnosis
of Moderate Mental Retardation. At present, she

is here on a voluntary basis. The patient has
previously exhibited hallucinations in the auditory sphere. The patient seemed to have improved and now she shows no overt delusions or
hallucinations. After a few weeks' stay in a
closed ward, because she has been behaving well,
partaking in ward activities, and helping in the
hospital chores, it was decided that she be
placed in an open ward. Patient is oriented in
all three spheres and memory for both recent and
remote events is intact. She has fair insight
and judgment. Patient has been going home regularly in the custody of her mother. There are
future plans for this patient either to stay
with her parents or to go to a rest home eventually. Medication: Stelazine, Artane, and
Thorazine.

CAROL'S BETHLEHEM DIARY

September 27

Today, at the heels of Mrs. Meredith, I saw the inside of Bethlehem State Hospital for the first time. Although little was said in the car on the way over, I knew I wasn't the only nervous one. I think the first things I observed on my tour of the hospital were the cleanliness and the tranquillity. The hospital certainly didn't measure up to the stereotypic vile madhouse that we have all seen in some old movie at one time or another. I did learn that in trying to accept people in institutions I had overcompensated in my expectations of normality. By saying that people in institutions are normal people who happen to have some problems, I somehow made myself believe that I would see no bizarre or irrational behavior. At one point on the tour, one of the girls in our group began to talk to the woman who was to be her patient. It was several minutes before I realized the irrationality of what the patient was saying. In fact, it was not until she looked out the window and said she saw Lassie coming that I realized she was not speaking in a completely rational manner.

Shortly before we were to leave I met the woman I am to work with, Jane. She is, as Mrs. Meredith says, obviously mentally retarded. Somehow this makes me feel less hopeful and enthusiastic about what I can hope to accomplish. Just before we left a man walked up and shook my hand. That was the first time I had ever touched a patient in a mental institution.

October 4

Today I spoke alone with Jane for the first time. My intentions were to try not to ask too many questions and to tell her about myself and how I happened to become a "volunteer" at Bethlehem. I did do just that, but our conversation remained quite strained and she seemed almost relieved when it was time for me to leave. There wasn't much give-and-take in the conversation. I did most of the initiation, although on a few occasions she did ask me questions. There were, however, many anxious

lulls in the conversation. We finally resorted to playing checkers at the end of our visit.

October 11

Today when I arrived she told me how sick she was--
the ailment, a small cut on her foot. However, when I
said that it was too bad because if she were feeling better we could have gone for a walk, she insisted that it
didn't really hurt that much and that we could go for a
walk anyway. Our walk gave me an opportunity to see that
she is an extremely childish person. Her sweet obedience
to the nurses and attendants is not a means she has found
to survive in the hospital but is a manifestation of her
childishness. Everything we encountered on our walk she
asked me to explain to her. She also initiated conversations with everyone we met along the way.

Away from the hospital we did manage to talk a little more easily. She told me a little about her past and
the special classes for the retarded that she attended
until she was seventeen. She also told me about her family and the fact that her father and mother have both
been ill recently. Since at twenty-seven she is the
youngest of several children, her parents are probably
rather old. This makes me fear that Jane will spend many
years to come in the hospital. Where do the retarded go
when they are not capable of independence but there is no
one to take care of them?

Jane talks of wanting to get a job. She has never
had one but she thinks she could be a housekeeper or
chambermaid because her mother taught her to do these
things. I think with some encouragement and an understanding employer she could hold a job, but I cannot
imagine her ever becoming independent and self-sufficient.

October 18

We were doing so well last week that today seems to
be a letdown. It wasn't a nice enough day to go outside
so we stayed in the hospital. I had noticed before that
Jane would begin to talk to herself at times in an inar-
ticulate and barely audible tone, but today she talked to

herself more than she talked to me. She even asked when
I was leaving, but when I said that if she didn't want to
talk to me any longer I would leave and come back another
day when she might feel more like having company, she insisted that I stay. I'm almost tempted to bring some
artsy-craftsy things just to help the hour pass. But
since she has shown me the artsy-craftsy things she has
done at the hospital, I don't really think this is what
she needs the most. If it were not for one occurrence at
the end of our visit I would think that she did want me
to stop coming, although she seems to try her best to
please me most of the time. Just as I was about to leave,
after saying good-bye to Jane and beginning to walk away
from her and out of the ward, a lady came up to me and
began talking rapidly and loudly, holding my hand while
walking beside me. Almost immediately Jane was back beside me competing for my attention.

October 25

        Today I had the good fortune to arrive at the hospi-
tal just as a Halloween party was beginning. Although I
didn't have much time to talk with Jane, I did get to observe some things about her and the hospital.

        Until now I had seen Jane as being somewhat aggres-
sive but I had failed to see the other side, the shy side.
At least six student nurses, sponsors of the party, asked
her to dance and she refused, saying she didn't want to,
although she knew how. Finally one of the student nurses
just dragged her out onto the floor and it was obvious
that she enjoyed every minute of it. This is making me
redo some thinking about forcing people into things. Because I hate being pushed into a situation, I usually try
not to force anyone else into a situation where they
might feel uncomfortable and embarrassed.

        Today I also had a chance to see just how condescend-
ing to patients the hospital can be. The whole party reminded me of a bunch of mothers trying to entertain their
four-year-olds. This was really brought home when a student nurse, mistaking me for a patient, came over and
asked me if I liked the music and if I would like to dance
with her. When I replied negatively on both counts she
left, probably to record me as an obstinate patient. My

only reaction was to be glad I was mistaken for a patient and not a nurse.

November 1

Today when I got to the hospital I found out that Jane would not be back from her weekend visit home until tonight. The trip was not wasted, however. Alicia managed to drag me off for a chat. The conversation was so bizarre that I'm still not sure exactly what went on. It was exactly the opposite of my situation with Jane. There were no lulls in this conversation and I was never in charge. In fact I never got a chance to initiate anything. By the end of our conversation, I almost felt as though she knew something I didn't know and she was laughing at me for being so stupid.

November 8

Today things went so well that I almost felt like a long-time friend catching up on things. Since we had not seen each other in two weeks we had a lot to tell each other. Then, because she is going to a party tonight, she asked me to set her hair. The most amazing thing we had to catch up on was Jane's move to the open ward. She says she likes it much better there, and indeed seems to like it better. I find this somewhat surprising since she seemed to thrive on the attention of the nurses and attendants and there is seldom one to be found on this ward.

Maybe I'll never see Jane leave the hospital but at least we are good friends. Perhaps that is something valuable.

November 15

I sometimes feel that I would like to bang Jane's head against a wall when she starts talking to herself. No matter what I do she continues to babble to herself. If I ignore the babbling she keeps right on doing it, and if I keep making her repeat what she is saying so that I

can understand it, she just gets annoyed and takes off
for the bathroom. I wish somehow I could make her see
that she has to stop talking to herself if she wants to
go home, which is what she keeps saying she wants to do.
Her babbling is usually accompanied by a smile. It's as
though she enjoys this special world more than the hospital, which is understandable. However, I wish I could
make her realize that she is going to have to cut this
behavior before she's able to leave the hospital.

November 22

Things seemed to be better today. Jane and I talked
more than usual. She seemed more willing to engage in
conversation with me than to talk to herself. She is excited about going home for Thanksgiving, in fact I almost
envy her because she has such a big, close family to go
home to. Now that I know more about her family circumstances I feel more hopeful about her release from the
hospital. They certainly don't seem to have put her here
because they don't want the responsibility of caring for
her.

November 29

Although I expected Jane to be excited and eager to
tell me about her vacation, I found her in bed and not
all that eager to get out of bed. In fact, she did her
best to avoid talking to me. Shortly after I arrived an
attendant began gathering people for a bingo game. Jane
immediately decided that she wanted to play. One of the
nurses said that she should talk to me since I had come
all the way out there. She almost looked thankful when
I insisted she play anyway. I think we both knew that we
had nothing to talk about while Jane was in this mood.

December 6

Jane was in bed again when I arrived today. Although she got up, she kept telling me how tired she was.
Although earlier in the semester I would have asked her
if she would like me to leave because I was afraid to

impose myself on her, I decided I was not going to let
her get rid of me today. We sat together yawning until
I finally asked her why she was tired, if she got enough
sleep at night. She assured me that she got enough sleep
but thought she was probably tired because she was sick.
Since she looks the picture of health, I asked if she was
really sick or perhaps just bored. She then admitted
that she was bored and we got to talking about the job
she once said she wanted to get. When I asked if she
would like a job in the hospital she said that she would
but didn't know how to get one. After leaving her I went
to see Mrs. Meredith about the job. A pleasant but over-
worked lady, she promised that she would bring it up at
some meeting that week.

December 13

     I arrived at the hospital today just as Jane was
leaving for work. I must admit I was amazed that the job
had come through so soon. Jane looked happier than I
have ever seen her. She was even apologetic about not
being able to visit with me. One of the nurses told me
that Jane had done well at her first day of work. Now
all I have to do is talk the hospital into paying some
commodity other than cigarettes. Jane doesn't smoke.

December 20

     The job seems to be agreeing with Jane. With talk-
ing about the job and the forthcoming holidays, she had
little time to fantasize. I just hope that this job is
what she needs to bring her back to reality. If she can
stop the fantasies, she may be on the way out of the hospital.

January 29

     It's been almost a month since I've seen Jane but it
doesn't seem to have hindered our relationship any. She
was in a very childish mood today, showing me all the
things she got for Christmas. She is still working and
says she likes it. She also seems interested in many

more things.   She is attending just about every social
function the hospital has.

February 1

     When I arrived at the hospital tonight, Jane was at
the Friday night dance. I watched from the side while
she danced with a fat, middle-aged man. She was beaming.
However, when he left her to dance with another woman,
she sat down and began a conversation with herself. This
is when I went over to her. She talked little to me all
evening. A man and woman were sitting together near us.
She jealously kept trying to gain the man's attention.
At one point in her mumbling she clearly said, "Jane, you
are going to get married." However, when I tried to pursue it she said she felt sick and wanted to go to bed.
Somehow I don't think working in a laundry is the career
she had in mind.

February 8

     Today I found Jane lying in her bed. When I asked
why, she said that she wasn't feeling well and that the
doctor said she was pregnant. A few of the ladies on the
ward corroborated this story while a few others called
her a liar. I went to see Mrs. Meredith to discuss what
had happened. It seems that while home for the weekend
she came up with this story and began to throw furniture
when anyone denied it. I'm glad I didn't deny it.

February 15

     Jane has forgotten she was pregnant and is working
again. She seems to be on a pretty even keel and even
talked to me almost as much as she talked to herself.
The hospital is the same as ever. Everyone's ready for a
big George Washington's birthday celebration. I wonder
how many of the ladies care which holiday it is; Jane
only cares about the food from the parties. Whoever co-
ordinates these parties must be a reject grade-school
teacher.

February 22

Jane was not exceedingly happy tonight. After she drank the Coke I bought her she began to look at the clock. She tried to convince me she didn't feel well by making eighteen trips to the bathroom so I finally suggested that I should leave. I feel as if she got the best of me in a game we are getting accustomed to playing. I don't want to force myself on her, however. Maybe I want her to say she doesn't want to see me instead of playing this sickness game. But why should I expect her to be honest when "normal" people play the headache game?

February 29

Jane was pretty relaxed tonight. She was happy and talkative but seems to be losing a little interest in her appearance. She has gained back some of the weight she lost in Weight Watchers, her hair was a mess, and her clothes crumpled.

March 7

She was sleeping by the time I arrived. I have, on occasion, awakened her in this situation. She is usually pretty aggravated and nervous when I do. I can't blame her. I dislike being awakened too.

March 14

Jane's pretty depressed. I tried to explain to her that I wouldn't see her for a few weeks because I was going to take a longer spring vacation than everyone else. I think she wished I had started my vacation a week earlier.

April 4

Jane was in a good mood. Things apparently went well at home on Easter weekend. She got lots of new clothes and lots of candy to help her outgrow them. She

is gaining weight but is concerned with her appearance.
She had me set her hair and she showed me the new dental
plate she got. This will definitely improve her appearance a great deal. There were some magazines around and
we started talking about reading. I know she can read a
little because I've heard her read signs around the hospital. However, when I suggested that I might bring her
some not very difficult things to read, she claimed she
didn't know how.

April 11

About five minutes after I arrived Jane decided she
was tired and wanted to go to bed. I was so aggravated
that I wanted to scream. I went to all the trouble of
getting out to the hospital and she didn't want to see
me. But I keep telling myself that I'm the one who initiated this relationship and I don't expect her to be
eternally grateful. She has the right to go to bed if
she wants to.

April 18

For the most part, I have always believed Jane but
it is getting to the point where I cannot. Her fantasies
are becoming indistinguishable from fact, although I used
to be able to tell them apart quite easily. Maybe she is
getting better at the game of convincing me that she is
something she really isn't.

April 25

I tried to explain to Jane that I would be leaving
soon but her only concern was whether or not I was getting
married after I graduate. She appears not to care that I
am leaving. I don't know if this indicates that the relationship didn't mean much to her, but it meant a great
deal to me. When I want to scream at the system and the
people who perpetuate it, it is not because of the masses
of people I know who don't belong there but because Jane
doesn't belong there. I could flatter myself into believing that she just doesn't want to show that she cares,

but I know Jane well enough to know that she doesn't hide
her feelings. I realized that she was more than just a
patient to me when I started feeling glad about people
asking if she was my sister. If there is one thing I can
ever accomplish I hope it is to find a place where people
like Jane can function without being locked up, conde-
scended to, and deprived of the right to be normal, dig-
nified individuals.

May 2

Jane and I said our good-byes today. Exams, graduation, and a multitude of other commitments are going to
scatter this person around for a while, so it seemed best
to part formally today rather than to chance just fading
away. It was simple and easy and I managed not to cry
until after I left the ward. I want to see her again.
But nothing would make me happier than to return to Bethlehem six months or a year from now and find her gone.

JANE FRANK

FOLLOW-UP INTERVIEW[1]

JP - So you remember Carol?

  Yes, how is she?

JP - I really don't know since she was not one
  of the students I myself had contact with.
  Perhaps we could start off a little differently....How long have you been here at the
  rest home?

  Since the summer.

JP - Could you tell me what you and Carol talked
  about?

  How I wanted to go home for good and
  how I wanted to get a job. That's all.

JP - What kind of a girl was Carol?

  She went to high school. I liked her.

JP - Did she tell you about herself?

  No....I like it better here than at the
  hospital. I have three friends here.
  That's all.

JP - You like to say "that's all."

  Yes. I'm going to Plattsburg tonight.
  That's where my mother, father, sister,
  and sister's little girl live.

JP - You smile when you talk of the little girl?

  I love her. But she was in an accident
  and cut her nose open.

JP - Was it bad?

  No. Not that bad.

JP - How long are you going to stay at home?

  Just two nights. I'll be back here

---

[1]Interviewed at rest home.

Sunday night.

JP - What do you do here?

I help do dishes and set the table.
Also I put the rubbish out for the
rubbish men.

JP - And what did you do at the hospital when
you were there?

Nothing. Eat breakfast, eat lunch, eat
supper, and go to bed. Sometimes I
stay up late here and watch television
and listen to the radio or records.

JP - Why did you go to the hospital in the first
place?

I don't know. No one told me that.

JP - Why do you think?

I don't know.

JP - Did you used to look forward to Carol's
visits?

Right.

JP - Did you used to talk with anyone besides
Carol at the hospital?

Only Carol, Mother, Father, Sister, and
sometimes the nurses and doctors. No
one else.

JP - How come you didn't talk with the other patients?

I don't know. They didn't tell me to.

JP - Did you get lonely at the hospital?

Not too much. If I did I'd call up my
mother or sister.

JP - Any regular visitors besides Carol?

No, only her.

JP - What would you talk with her about?

I forget now.

JP - Do you remember anything that happened between you and her?

    No.

JP - Would you like to see her again?

    Right....Is she still home? I think
she went home once for Christmas and
then she came back.

JP - You remember saying goodbye to her?

    Right. (Long pause)

JP - What are you thinking about?

    I'm happy because I'm going to be going
home in the morning?

JP - You know you keep mumbling to yourself
while I take notes. Why do you do that?

    I don't know. I just do it.

JP - What do you say to yourself?

    Not too much. I can't....

JP - Do you hear voices too?

    Right.

JP - What do the voices say?

    I don't know. They're not in here now.
They went home. I shouted for them to
go home. Sometimes I yell at them.
Not too much though.

JP - What do the voices say exactly?

    Go home with my mother. Help my father
and my sister.

JP - Are the voices real?

    Yes.

JP - Who are they?

    Boys and girls.

JP - People you've known?

    Right.

JP - They keep you company?

    Right.

JP - Ever tell Carol about the voices?

    Yes.

JP - What did she say?

    She said not to talk to them. Tell
    them to go home and stay home...but
    I hear them anyway.

JP - Constantly?

    Yes.

JP - Are they friendly?

    Sometimes yes and sometimes no. Some-
    times they say nasty words at me. "Get
    the hell home and stay home! Go and
    get married! Go stay with Mother and
    Father, Sister and Brother!"

JP - What would you want if you had one wish?

    I wish to be married.

JP - Ever have a boyfriend?

    I have three of them.   (Holding up
    three of her fingers)

JP - Real ones or only in your head?

    Real ones. One was going to give me
    a ten-cent ring, but I told him to give
    me a real one. He was a boyfriend at
    the hospital. He was nice to me. He'd
    get me pizza pies, ice cream cones,
    grinders, and everything. But I can't
    see him now. He's probably married to
    someone else. I'm not at Bethlehem
    anymore.

JP - You miss him?

    He was nice. He had long hair and
    everything.

JP - What was he doing in the hospital?

He was a doctor. A single doctor.

JP - Did you ever kiss him?

Yes. A long time ago. Then the nurse
spanked me. I don't know why.

JP - Did the doctor want you to kiss him?

No. He locked me in my room after that
for five days.

JP - Ever tell Carol about this?

No, I didn't. She didn't ask me it.

JP - What did you tell Carol that you haven't
told me?

I can't tell you.

JP - What kind of girl was she?

She had slacks and nice clothes on.
That's all. One time before Christmas
she took me to the university and
showed me all the buildings and even
took me into one of them.

JP - What impressed you about the university?

I saw where they eat, where they sleep,
where they took baths, and where they
put the cars away.

JP - Did you like that?

Yes. She asked me if I wanted to go to
that school--first I said yes and then
I said no. I really do want to go to
school. But there are too many hippies
at that school. They won't take baths
or anything.

JP - Anyone in your family go to college?

My sister and my brother used to.

JP - How come they did and you didn't?

I don't know. They used to kick me off
the bus. I don't know why.

JP - Is it because you're not as smart as other

people?

Right.

JP - Do you feel bad about that?

No.

JP - What do you feel bad about?

Not too much. I'm happy here.

JP - Would you change places with Carol?

Right. I really wish I could but I can't, huh?

JP - Why would you want to change with her?

I'd like to go back to school. I wish there was a new school around here that could take me. (Pause)

JP - Does Carol have a boyfriend?

She has two. But I have three. I once asked her and she told me that she had two.

JP - Is Carol a pretty girl?

Yes, she is.

JP - Do you think she liked you?

Yes, she used to take me shopping. Used to get me grinders, pizza, potato chips, root beer, cocoa, peanuts, milkshakes.

JP - I guess you love to eat.

Yes, very much.

JP - Is that the most important thing to you in life?

Yes....You know I have a student now too--Bess. But lately she's been sick in bed.

JP - I guess we'd better stop talking soon. So you like the student program?

Oh yes! They're very nice to me.

JP - Could we make it better?

      Maybe.

JP - How?

      I don't know.

JP - O.k. Thanks for talking with me.

4

MY LITTLE QUIET CORNER

Karen and Alicia

Haley (1959) has characterized the three basic approaches to understanding schizophrenic behavior as the classical, intrapsychic, and interpersonal. In the classical approach, the examiner attempts to determine whether the person is in contact with reality, and odd behavior is attributed to organic pathology. The intrapsychic approach centers around the person's thought processes, and attempts to unravel the person's psychological history and the symbolic meanings of his thinking and fantasy. The interpersonal approach emphasizes observable interaction between the person and others, and may reveal the kind of learning situation that might have produced the behavior in question. Laing (1967), representing the latter school of thought, writes on the subject of the schizophrenic experience, "...we may well ask why these people have to be, often brilliantly, so devious, so elusive, so adept at making themselves unremittingly incomprehensible."

Alicia intimidated people with her intelligence and rapid, often apparently illogical, conversation. One outstanding quality of Alicia's communications was that she was committed to none of them--she could always deny the meaning given to them if she were "put on the spot." One way of looking at communication (Watzlawick *et al.*, 1967) is to note that it always defines the sender's view of his relationship with the receiver; even asking some-

one for a match with which to light a cigarette carries
the message, "This is a relationship in which I may request something." It has been suggested that the schizophrenic is responding to the dilemma of commitment to
another person implied by any communication; because of
past learning contexts (see Bateson *et al*., 1956) the
person feels "put on the spot" in any interpersonal situation. In a desperate attempt not to communicate, the
schizophrenic denies that he is communicating. That
I / am saying something / to you / in this situation may
be denied four times, each time so fantastically that
the denial itself is denied (Haley, 1959): the person may
use an alias or be a victim of voices, alcohol, drugs, or
insanity itself; he may speak in an incomprehensible word
salad, contradict his statements, or call himself a liar;
he may say the person to whom he speaks is someone else,
perhaps an FBI agent, or speak to an imaginary person;
and he may claim to speak of another time or in another
place.

Consider this provocative framework as you encounter
Alicia, who says of herself, "I speak in poetry." Note,
too, the ingredients of Karen and Alicia's relationship.
In the previous chapter, Carol mentioned her one meeting
with Alicia, saying, "By the end of our conversation, I
almost felt as though she knew something I didn't know
and she was laughing at me for being so stupid." Karen,
too, was frightened of Alicia--of being rejected, of saying the wrong thing, and of being controlled by her.
Early in the year she realized her own need to relate to
Alicia and was afraid of making a mistake, thereby losing
her; she, too, was in a struggle for control of the relationship.

It is useful to think about the possible reasons why
Karen and the other students at times seem so worried
that the patient they have been assigned will reject them.
Karen overcame this somewhat as she and Alicia became
closer during the year. Follow the relationship developing between Alicia and Karen and try to identify the
major problems Karen attempts to cope with at each stage--
for example, fear of rejection and fear of doing harm at
the beginning of the relationship. Notice how Karen's
initial hopes--for a strong friendship, and for great
progress in completely clearing up Alicia's problems--
are slow to change and how this leaves her vulnerable

to her own widely fluctuating moods. Should Karen have been more realistic in her aspirations and goals? Would a clearer separation between herself and Alicia have been more beneficial to them both? How would you have communicated with Alicia?

BETHLEHEM STATE HOSPITAL

MEDICAL RECORD

Alicia Miller   Patient #70103

ADMISSION NOTE - APRIL 18, 1965

This white, single, female patient...states that she was in several hospitals before, but does not know why....Patient said that she was under the care of a psychiatrist for twenty-six years; actually, the patient is only twenty-six years old. When this examiner asked how she could be under a psychiatrist's care for that length of time, patient answered, "Yes, I even remember when my mother bore me. I remember such difficulty."

Then she asked this examiner why everything she said was written down and would it be used against her. She also seems to be confused in religious matters. During the conversation she cried a lot....

MAY 18, 1965   Staff Summary: This case was diagnosed as Schizophrenic Reaction, Acute Undifferentiated Type.

NOVEMBER 14, 1965   Absence to November 18, 1965. Condition: Improved. Care of mother. Patient can go for the holiday. Doing better. Librium and Benadryl.

ADMISSION NOTE - DECEMBER 14, 1967

This twenty-eight-year-old, single, female patient, accompanied by her parents, was admitted today for the second time at 4:00 p.m.

According to the legal paper, "Patient has been excited and uncontrolled. Visited cousin in Bentree and left in the middle of the night. She has fantasies of a sexual nature. Her train of thought is illogical and almost incoherent."

129

FEBRUARY 11, 1968   INTERVAL CLINICAL SUMMARY
This was the second admission of this twenty-
eight-year-old, single, female patient who came
to our hospital on December 4, 1967....

In March, 1963, the patient started with a
nervous breakdown at college from which she recovered although she continued on medication.
Hospitalization was necessary on several occasions since March, 1963, the patient recovering
in each instance and being maintained on medication and psychiatric care. The first mental
hospitalization was at Eastern Mountain in April,
1963. The second mental disturbance occurred in
April, 1965. At that time she became highly
nervous and agitated, started praying, became
restless and difficult to reason with. According
to her mother's information, she was living in a
world of fantasy, could not face up to reality,
lacked self-confidence, was difficult to reason
with, and started wandering back and forth to
neighbors. At our hospital the diagnosis of
Acute Schizophrenic Episode was given.

COURSE IN THE HOSPITAL   After the first few days
the patient still appeared tense, restless, apprehensive, and in obvious discomfort at being
brought to this institution against her will.
She tried to rationalize as much as possible her
commitment to our institution. Embitteredly,
she blamed her parents, especially her mother,
accusing her of not comprehending her delicate
and special problems in such a critical period
of her life. Also, she vehemently blamed both
her parents, portraying them as being strictly
puritanical New England people, possessive, demanding, domineering, whose excessive, severe
discipline created in the patient a great amount
of hatred and resentment, instead of love and
affection. During several interviews she appeared somewhat agitated, irritable, her emotions once again being under very fragile control. She burst into tears easily, her facial
expression disclosing a sort of melancholy and,
at times, very black pessimism. Under the effects of medication she recovered quite quickly

from her acute psychotic episode. She spoke
rationally and developed very slight insight
into her present nervous condition. She spoke
with enthusiasm about the future, about her plan
for further studies at college in order to become a teacher.

On the ward it was said that she resented
discipline and appeared hostile, demanding, and
difficult to reason with. She would share the
confidence of very few patients, although she
was preoccupied, depressed, sad, and tearful at
intervals. Personal hygiene appeared impeccable
for the second part of her sojourn at our hospital. Sleeping and eating habits were satisfactory.

On December 13, 1967, she was released,
condition improved, in care of her mother.

MARCH 17, 1968   This patient was visited today
by her mother and father and did not seem at all
pleased either with their visit or what they
said during it. This patient was heard to
scream both at the mother and father that she
wanted to leave here. When interviewed shortly
thereafter by this examiner, she claimed that
she would like to leave the institution at this
time. She was persuaded not to. Her condition
has improved considerably over the past week;
she had been convinced she saw a vision of a
tall standing man whose feet did not touch the
ground, and she mentioned other ideas of this
nature. Now her judgment and insight have progressed to the point where she looks upon these
ideas skeptically. It was felt, however, that
said condition, in spite of having improved, was
not sufficient to warrant release from the institution at this time. The patient then agreed
that she is not opposed to staying here for a
few days longer.

MARCH 30, 1968   This patient was seen almost
every day since the 17th of March, 1968, during
which period noticeable improvements had been
made. Patient looked forward to leaving this

institution and had plans for pursuing the study
of Chinese more assiduously and in a more comfortable environment. Toward the end of this
period of observation, however, the patient began talking of her love for "Albert" and of
being loved by "John." Her thoughts were di-
rected more towards the former. The patient
feels that she owes this Albert a lot and he,
her. She was quite annoyed at the thought of
having to remain here for another thirty days or
so (it would appear that her parents had granted
permission for a longer stay at this institution).
The patient felt that it would be a waste of time
doing so, and it would contribute more to her
downfall than to her improvement. This morning,
this examiner found the patient playing the piano.
When he approached, what he thought to have been
singing was crying. The patient on seeing this
examiner became quite angry, saying, "If you have
any pull or connections, why don't you get me out
of here. I see no reason why I should be kept
here." Asked if she was angry, the patient replied in the affirmative. Later that day the
patient signed a voluntary paper. She was then
granted a visit and was released to the custody
of her mother and father. The patient was given
an appointment to return to see this examiner.
Her condition at the time of release: Improved.

APRIL 15, 1968   This patient was seen and interviewed today on the admission ward. She laughed
inappropriately several times. She felt that she
could do something for one of the other patients
here by operating on her heart. She also felt
that she was an astronaut and she would go not to
the moon, but in the area of the moon and from
there to Mars. She also stated that there was a
bear around her house and that once when she and
her dog went out for a walk, the dog stood up on
his hind legs because he saw this bear. Asked
whether or not she had seen this bear, she said,
"No," but she imagined it was there. The patient,
at the present time, is not at all well.

MAY 20, 1968   Returned from visit by a friend.

Patient very deluded and hallucinated. Claims she is a nun and had seen visions of Christ and Our Blessed Lady. Blessed Lady told her, "Don't be afraid." Patient laughs inappropriately. She is mentally confused, vague, and irrelevant.

AUGUST 2, 1968   This patient reported to this institution today in an agitated, overtalkative, overactive state. When she was pressured into the office of this examiner, the patient raised her arms like a flamenco dancer. She shouted a few words with a Spanish intonation, clapping her hands together. She then said, "Olé." Offered a seat, the patient declined at first and after a moment of standing still, she sat on the desk beside this examiner. Then she said to the examiner, "What makes you think that you might be the Devil's advocate? I could pass psychiatry very easily, but I don't want to be a psychiatrist." ...She would jump to the subject of astronauts, etc., all in one breath....It was recommended that the patient remain at this institution because of her condition....

SEPTEMBER 15, 1968   The patient returned to this institution August 27, 1968, upon insistence of parents. After spending a week at home doing well, she suddenly began staring into space, talking to herself. Her mother stated that this behavior followed soon after the patient reread several letters from an old sweetheart. Shortly thereafter she began acting strangely: looking into space, talking to herself in a loud voice, etc. She then apparently began walking the streets, arrived at a friend's home where she took off her blouse. Then she left and continued to walk through the streets. She allegedly stated that if men could walk the streets seminude, so could she. She arrived at someone else's home, requesting to lie in that person's bed. She stayed there one hour and left. She finally was overtaken and yelled when it was requested that she return to the hospital.

OCTOBER 16, 1968   This patient returned to the

hospital today after almost fourteen days at
home. During her stay at home, she reported at
least three times to this examiner. Today, no
sooner had the patient arrived on the ward than
she let out a scream which frightened everyone.
Asked why she had done this, the patient said
that the fire alarm had just sounded, so she
thought she could do the same thing. The patient insists that she has been raped. It was
difficult to accept the patient's word at this
time in view of her mental status. This matter
will be taken up with her at a later date.

NOVEMBER 15, 1968   The patient gave as a reason
for being back here that she had an altercation
with her father and, "I had to use the high
karate." The patient continued to say that, "My
father wanted to slit me in half." In this tone
of voice, the patient continued the story by
saying that her father is going into space and
doesn't want her to be a space woman, etc....An
incident which led to her return to this institution occurred when the patient went downstairs
at her parents' home where she was residing,
took dishes, and smashed them one at a time on
the floor. It would appear that the patient
planned on returning for more dishes, but she
was stopped by her father. It was then that the
altercation ensued.

APRIL 15, 1969   Patient has gained an insight
into her mental condition. She wants to go home.
She said she couldn't be a nun because of her
emotional problem and she cannot financially af-
ford to be a doctor. She is given ground privileges.

JULY 28, 1969   At present, this patient wants
to be discharged from the hospital. She is hopeful she can find a job outside, be able to maintain an apartment, and live by herself. She
also wants to go back to the university to finish her college degree. She has been persuaded
she is not quite ready for all of this. She has
been referred for job placement. Alicia has

improved, but she is not well enough to realize
that there are limitations to what she can do
and take. She could be easily provoked, could
easily get emotional over any unusual or disturbing event in the ward. Patient needs further hospitalization.

AUGUST 7, 1970   ANNUAL NOTE   Voluntary admission. Chronic case. Diagnosed as Schizophrenia,
Schizo-Affective Type. Tends to have mood
swings from depression to elation, accompanied
by delusions. Says at times she is a nun, at
times a nurse, other times claims she is a saint.
She has poor insight and judgment. She is on
Triavil and also Valium for anxiety. In spite of
patient's high intelligence, she offers the picture of an immature, insecure, and frustrated
young woman, striving for independence, disobey-
ing her parents' discipline, blaming and resent-
ing her parents' attitude toward her. She burst
into tears easily while trying to explain to
examiner the reasons for her second commitment
to the hospital. She vehemently blamed her parents, portraying them as being strict, possessive, puritanical New England people. Their
excessive, severe discipline alienated the
patient who, for years, had been unsuccessfully
striving for independence. She says, "I would
like to have my little way of life, my little
quiet corner."

KAREN'S BETHLEHEM DIARY

September 27

This afternoon we had our tour of the hospital and also were introduced to our patients.

The grounds and outside appearance of Bethlehem are really impressive and very beautiful. Inside is another story. Although not as bad as I expected, the halls were dingy and everything looked quite old and used. It all had that awful "hospital smell."

We had a short meeting in the auditorium where we met the head nurse, Mrs. Olsen, the social worker, Mrs. Meredith, and the psychologist, Mrs. Kennedy. Then we said our names and were assigned our patients. When I said my name, Mrs. Olsen said, "This is the one." Then they had a little conference and decided finally to give me my person anyway, Alicia Miller.

Then we went on our tour. We were in groups of four and our group was headed by Mrs. Meredith. The wards were not as bad as I expected, but bad enough. The only ward which exhibited any real activity was the women's open. The people there would easily have passed as normal. The women's admissions is where my patient was located (most girls were assigned here too). The rooms are so tiny and dull--I would hate to live there. Another student said to imagine if we were put in for forty days while we thought we were sane--I'd go "crazy," I really would. A lot of the people just sit and shake or rock or pace up and down the halls. To me, many of the patients on the ward looked retarded. Maybe it's just the dull look in everyone's face.

My person was in the OT room. When we walked in, three people were there: a man, a young woman, and an old lady. I figured my patient was the old lady; however, I was wrong. Alicia was the girl sitting with the man. Mrs. Meredith introduced me and Alicia asked if I wanted to see the poem she was writing. She also said she was going to have her poems published and offered the group a bunch of photographs to look through. She appeared extremely bright and intelligent. As I sat down she said, "I speak in poetry so we may have trouble talking." I said something to the effect that, well, we'd see what

136

would happen. Then she started to explain her poem to
the group. It was extremely strange--although she didn't
get a chance to finish explaining it. She said that
there was a boy, Robert, who should be in college or a
Rhodes scholar, but who was only in third grade because
he was sort of retarded. She mentioned something about
picking him up off the ground, holding him, and then he
was all right. She also said that she spoke Chinese and
that so did Robert and sometimes they'd go to the White
House and speak Chinese there. Another part of her poem
had Lassie in it. Suddenly she turned to the window
after mentioning something about Lassie, and said, "Look--
here comes Lassie now!" I asked her if it was o.k. if I
came on Wednesday afternoons. She said o.k., but....Then
she ran over to one of the other girls in our group and
said that she wanted to work with her. The other girl
explained that it was impossible and that I was assigned
to work with her. She came back, looked at me, and finally said, "That's o.k., it'll be all right." I told her
I'd see her next week and then we went on. I'm glad she
seems so bright and talkative, but I am a bit afraid of
how I should respond to her "delusions." There could be
some truth in them, but perhaps she's just testing me as
described in Umbarger's book, *College Students in a Mental Hospital*. I'll really have to think about how I will
respond before next week. Maybe the group will have some
suggestions. One of the students who worked at Bethlehem
last year said he thought that she was only showing off
and acting especially strange for the group's benefit or
for attention's sake. This may be true.

We toured the rest of the hospital. It's pretty depressing. Some people complained to Mrs. Meredith about
being put on locked wards when they hadn't done anything
wrong--it was really pathetic. It really makes you want
to help--if you can.

It seems as if this is going to be an extremely interesting and valuable experience for me. I hope it is
for Alicia, too.

October 6

The time with Alicia went extremely quickly today.
It was really great. When I arrived Alicia was with her

mother. She told me to go into the OT room and draw a
rose. I went in and she had watercolors, crayons, and
paper set up. So I painted a rose. The man in the OT
room, Mr. Gordon, said that I could expect a great improvement in Alicia in about two weeks or so. It seems
she goes through cycles of being very bad (usually right
after being home) to being very good (then she's allowed
to go home for a visit and the cycle starts again). I
wonder if home is the true problem. Her mother seems
quite concerned, but they probably just aren't on the
same level.

When Alicia first came into the OT room she was loud
and excited like she was last time. She was kidding Mr.
Gordon and also me. She spoke of what "schizy" is and
paranoid. Her definition of paranoid was correct and she
said that she wasn't--that people really had been chasing
her. She said one was schizy if one gossiped too much.
I just sort of said uh-huh and didn't comment. She drew
two good pictures of roses for me and signed them. She
put a "joke" in Chinese on the bottom of one. She
wouldn't tell me what it said, though.

We eventually went into her room and she showed me
her Chinese and Japanese books. I couldn't believe that
she really spoke Chinese--I thought she had been bull-
shitting me the week before--but she can speak Chinese,
Japanese, French, German, and Russian. She's quite an
amazing and intelligent person. She also showed me her
book of photographs--her family, school friends, boyfriends, etc. She mentioned one boy who had been killed
in an airplane crash and said that this had to do with
the beginning of her problem--I wonder whether this is
true. She also spoke briefly of her problems with her
parents, brothers, and sisters. She said that they can't
understand her creativity and that they also are competing with her on that and all levels. She seems to
feel that most of her problem comes from her home and
family--she implied this to me right in front of her
mother. It seems that she might be putting her problems'
causality onto others instead of trying to cope with
whatever it is within herself. Most people use this defense automatically. Maybe I can question her about it.

She does make me a little nervous still. She seems
more intelligent than I am and she seems to be trying to

take control of the relationship and trying to counsel me, rather than letting me try to help her. I hope we can find a level of some kind of symbiotic relationship.

The rest of the session was spent talking about things like the university, school in general, gaining weight, the other patients, and a million other topics (it seemed).

Another thing threw me--when I was leaving and mentioned that I would be back at the same time next week, Alicia said that she didn't know if she'd be there, because she was unsure and might be doing other things. I don't know what she meant by that--we'll see!

I think I will try to bring something for us to do next week and see how she accepts that.

October 13

Alicia was resting when I got there, but got up and came out of her room. She was dressed really nicely and said she was waiting for her parents to pick her up to take her home. This shook me up a little because I wasn't really sure that I could believe her, but I didn't want to doubt her as I had about her speaking Chinese. I was pretty sure she wouldn't try to fool me. Also she had all her things packed up. She said she was supposed to have left the day before but that no one had come to get her and that they then said they'd come in the morning but they hadn't. I guess that's what made me doubt her at all--I couldn't believe, if she really was getting out, that her parents wouldn't come get her as soon as possible. But perhaps this is how her family operates. If so, then I think perhaps it's a great deal of Alicia's problem. If they couldn't understand how much she'd be itching to get out--then I guess they just can't understand people. I think it was really cruel to make her wait and especially not to let her know if they were coming at all. She must have tried calling home about five times while we were downstairs, but no one was home.

Alicia was pretty down as a result of all this. She didn't talk very much except when I started a conversation, but she was very apologetic about being quiet and explained how she had been all set to go yesterday and

had been waiting ever since. I understood why completely
so I just questioned her about things like: what she'd do
when she got home, where she lives, how she thought she'd
do out of the hospital, etc. I sort of adopted her mood.
I felt depressed and apprehensive and also thought that
it was very unfair for her parents not to have come for
her. So we shared moods for awhile without too much conversation. We exchanged addresses and Alicia said she'd
write and let me know if she went home or not. I heard
today in discussion group that she did leave. I'm happy
for her, but sad because I had really looked forward to
working with her for a whole year. I felt we could have
been good friends and made a lot of progress in completely clearing up Alicia's problem. I just hope things go
well for Alicia and that it isn't necessary for her to
come back.

October 20

    I found out early Wednesday that Alicia did not go
home last week so I went to see her. I brought her a
book and a pumpkin.

    She was waiting downstairs for me--very dressed up
and looking very nice.

    I gave her the book and pumpkin and I think she was
very impressed that I had spent money to get her something.

    We had a good talk again, discussing her plans for
getting out and working, etc. She said she believed she
would be getting out Friday, but when I called her home
tonight her mother said she was still in the hospital--
that they had met with the doctor and decided that it
would be best for Alicia to stay in the hospital until
she could go to a halfway house or an apartment. They
feel she should not go home.

    I got to meet two other patients from the hospital--
Arthur and some other boy. We had interesting conversations. Arthur seemed really nice, but shy. The other
guy was really nice too. It is hard to believe that you
are in a hospital when you talk to people like that.
It's hard to understand why they are there.

This week when I go to see Alicia I think maybe we can make some plans for working out what she'll be doing so she can get out soon--I know that's what she really wants to do.

October 27, October 29, November 3

When I went up on the ward October 27th, I found that Alicia had had a relapse and that she was on the back ward in seclusion. I was really shocked and didn't quite know what to do or say. I had assumed that we could spend our time discussing apartment hunting, jobs, etc. Then I was faced with the prospect of seeing a "really crazy" person. Alicia was in pretty bad shape-- a bundle of motion, nerves, and words. I was really overwhelmed and even though she is acting much better now, I'm still sort of wary of her and upset about it. That first time (October 27), Alicia said a lot of crazy things but I felt she really didn't have any control over what she was saying--so I listened intently and tried to figure out what she was saying to me through it all. I really did think she was trying to tell me something through her tales and rambling.

I felt really bad when I had to leave that first time and Alicia seemed to want me to stay, so I said I'd go back on Friday and I did.

Alicia wasn't as confused, shaky, or full of motion as she had been before, but she was still speaking of Saturn and other things. We went outside and Alicia wanted to run away to the university. I told her we couldn't do that, but that when she got out she could certainly come over to visit and we'd go to classes and things. I was still treating her like a China doll--if I said or did something to disturb her she'd get super upset and either regress or get mad at me and consequently our relationship would be ruined. I guess I am really afraid of ruining our relationship for two reasons: (1) it would be bad for Alicia and (2) it would be bad for me. I guess I sort of feel I need her to an extent too--so I don't want to do anything to get her mad at me. I think that now I should be a little more strong with her, however, because it'll be good for her, for our relationship, and for me because I'm usually not like that.

This last time that I saw Alicia she seemed a lot better, but she still spoke to me of Saturn, writing plays, etc. It seems more and more that she doesn't have to say these things to me, but she does anyway. I don't know if I should confront her or not. We talked about it a bit in discussion group today and the opinion was divided. But I think most people felt that I should tell her in some subtle way that I don't really believe she's going to go to Saturn, but that she certainly seems to know a lot about it; or when she talks about plays, say something like--I'd think you were creative even if you didn't write *Hair*. These seem like really good suggestions and though I'll be afraid to try them I'm going to attempt it on Wednesday.

People seem to be getting a bit discouraged about their work now, so we also talked about that in discussion today. We sort of figured out that those people who were getting discouraged were those who had placed their goals too high. They had goals such as getting their patients out of the hospital, or into an open ward and ready to go out--sort of a complete cure goal. The others who were not hoping for such things but just trying to form the best relationships possible seemed to feel they were quite successful and were satisfied and happy with their progress. So perhaps it would be best for us to lower our expectations because then we would be less frustrated and thus be more successful in our work. Of course it wouldn't be good to completely disregard any chance for our patients' release, but at the same time I think it would do both the "patients" and students good to put a reasonable limit on their expectations.

I'm going to try to do that with Alicia. I want to get her out, but I'm not going to *expect* that I will-- I'll still try, but I won't be as disappointed if problems arise. I'm going to try to work more on developing a close interpersonal relationship with her.

November 10, November 17

Last week Alicia and I went downtown, without per-

mission, and ate the pizza I promised her. We had an interesting time. Alicia talked a lot about her background
and told me some pretty personal things. I promised I
wouldn't tell anyone so I won't write about it here. I
was pretty surprised that she had told me these things,
but I figured she trusted me enough to confide in me.
Alicia was pretty shaky while we were downtown, but she
controlled herself well. It made me feel really sad to
see the longing way in which she looked at college students and their boyfriends. She looked awfully sad, but
she seemed to enjoy the afternoon very much.

This week Alicia and I just stayed in her room and
talked. We talked about this psychology course, the hospital, how bad it is for the patients, old times, boyfriends, etc. I really felt that we were making progress
in becoming closer. She has started to tell me things
which, in context, can be seen as leading to or contrib-
uting to her "illness."

Then Wednesday night the class was supposed to meet
at Bethlehem and get some of the patients to go to the
square dance. No one showed up so Mary, my roommate, and
I spent our time talking to Alicia. It was pretty
strange. It seems to me that she talks a little differently from when she is with me alone. But she seemed to
talk about the same things which really shocked me. She
told Mary (and the rest of the ward due to her loudness)
the same personal things she made me promise not to tell
anyone. I was sort of mad and pretty hurt, I guess. I
felt that what she had been telling me was important and
that she wouldn't go around telling everyone these things.
By telling Mary she made me feel that our relationship
really isn't as valuable or important or special to her
as it is to me. This really upset me. I didn't confront
her about it, but maybe I will on Monday when I go to see
her.

One other thing that bothered me about Wednesday
night's meeting was that Alicia, in answer to Bill
Fremouw's comment that he hoped he'd get a chance to talk
to her next time, answered that no, he wouldn't because
she wouldn't be there--that she was going home for good
right after Thanksgiving. This really surprised me too,
because she hadn't mentioned anything about it to me that
afternoon or evening. Then later, when she was talking

to Mary and me about making a long skirt, I said that
after Thanksgiving I'd bring my sewing machine and maybe
we could do it together. She curtly replied that no, she
wouldn't be there. This scares me because it seems to be
the exact same thing she started doing about two or three
weeks before she had her "setback." It seems that the
cycle is starting over again and I really wonder if there
is anything I can do to stop it. I'm going to talk to
Mrs. Meredith before I see Alicia on Monday to see if it
is true that she's leaving and if not I'll have to confront her about that too.

November 22

    I tried to see Mrs. Meredith before I went to see
Alicia, but she wasn't in. I did talk to the young nurse
on the ward before I saw Alicia and she said that Alicia
was depressed because the doctor wouldn't let her stay
home for two weeks--he'd only let her go for four days.

    I talked to Alicia and she was depressed. She had
wanted to be home for two weeks so she'd have a chance to
look for a job and an apartment. She feels that Mrs.
Meredith and Mr. Winston really don't do too much for
her--that she must do it for herself. I said that I
would try to speak to them for her after Thanksgiving.
So this explained why she told Bill that she wasn't going
to be in the hospital after the vacation. That was what
she was trying for.

    We talked awhile and went and got hot chocolate.
She said she'd be seeing an old boyfriend over the vacation, doing shopping, etc., but she didn't seem over-
enthused about going home. It seemed to me that she
wanted to be out, but not necessarily at home or in that
type of situation. She seemed apprehensive.

    I was worried because of what the nurse and everyone
else had said: that when Alicia goes home she comes back
worse off than ever. So I tried to feel Alicia out about
whether or not she thought going home upset her. She
didn't really give me a straight answer. I think that's
because she knows it does upset her, but she wants to get
out anyway and this is the only way she can.

    I just told her to try to keep calm and not to get

upset while she's home and she said she'd try, but I was pretty convinced that after Thanksgiving I'd be seeing a very upset, messed-up Alicia. The thought depresses and frustrates me--what can I do about it?

December 1

I found Alicia in the condition I expected. She was all over the place--physically, mentally, and emotionally. I was really sad and frustrated to see her like this again. Also our meeting in and of itself was very frustrating. I think Alicia was worse when I left than when I first arrived. I think she expected me to be nonbothersome, to laugh and be crazy along with her. Instead I tried to understand what she was saying and asked her questions, etc. So she classified me as she does the rest of the hospital staff--as unwilling to help or understand her. This hurts me because I feel that I've been trying to be a lot better to Alicia than the hospital staff. I guess I'm not succeeding as far as she's concerned.

I really don't know what comes next. I've been trying so hard, but it seems to have done no good. I just hope that in the future I can communicate to Alicia just how much I care and that I do want to understand and be able to communicate with her--even when she's upset. I just want her to know that and not to feel that I'm only trying to psych her out for my own selfish purposes. I only hope I can let her know and that she believes me.

December 8

Same as above, unfortunately.

December 15

I spent most of my time with Mrs. Kennedy talking about Alicia. She said she had spoken to Alicia the day before and that she was doing better. She said she offered her help, but Alicia just said she wanted to take some psychological tests.

I asked Mrs. Kennedy if she thought there was some way that I could get permission for Alicia to take a course at the college with me. With her help I got it o.k.'d through Dr. Rakosky. So I guess not everyone who works at the hospital is against me. I was sure it would take much more than a five minute chat to convince anyone.

When I did see Alicia I had woken her up so she wasn't too enthusiastic about my plan. Also she said that by then Mr. Winston might have a foster home for her--wishful thinking, I'm afraid. I was disappointed at her reaction--I guess I expected great excitement because I was so excited. Well, we'll see what happens at the beginning of next semester. If Alicia is still at the hospital I'm sure she will be excited about getting out for a while, "x" times a week.

Christmas Vacation

I got the surprise of my life when I picked up the phone one morning last week. It was Alicia! I had told her that if she felt she needed me while she was home to call me, but I never thought she would.

She sounded o.k. for part of the conversation, but not too good for the rest. That didn't upset me too much--I was so happy that she felt she could trust me enough to call me when she needed me. The call was short because she called collect and didn't want to spend my money, but it was well worth it to me. I'm going to see her tomorrow.

February 24

So much has happened since I last wrote in this journal,[1] but Alicia's condition now is the same as

---

[1]Supplementary note, January, 1974. When I got to the ward that day I looked for Alicia, but didn't see her, so I asked the nurse on duty where she was. The nurse told me that she was over in the infirmary. She told me that Alicia had become unmanageable and had been

always. The cycle continues--there's got to be something
to break it--I refuse to accept the possibility that
Alicia will be in Bethlehem for the rest of her life--I
just will not believe it--how can that happen and why
should it be?

The infirmary thing seemed like it should have been
a turning point. After going all the way back she should
come out and be o.k. Why can't saying it make it true in
this case? Things can't get much worse than they were
last time--there's no direction to go but up, is there?--
obviously not. She's not as bad as she was, but she's
not o.k. I'm really getting depressed about her chances.

---

put on Ward Three. After being put there Alicia had
stopped eating, drinking, going to the bathroom, and
taking medications--she had completely shut down her
system.

After several days Alicia became physically ill and
so they had transferred her to the infirmary. I was
granted permission to see her there. Alicia was in very
bad shape. They were feeding her intravenously and she
was in restraints--her arms and legs tied to the bed
frame. She didn't open her eyes or give any signs of
recognizing me or of being aware that I was even there.
I went to visit her several times a week while she was
there. She started to be more aware of her surroundings
and started to tell me her side of the story. She had
not wanted to return to the hospital and had decided that
she would rather die than continue her existence at Bethlehem any longer. So she shut herself down and tried to
die--the hospital interfered. She claimed that despite
the hospital's attempts to save her she had, indeed, died
and she was finding it difficult to come back to life
after that death. I spent as much time with her as I
could stand. Alicia was upsetting enough, but the infirmary environment and what I saw, heard, smelled, and
felt there was more than I could take. Alicia spent
about three weeks in the infirmary and was then released
to the ward.

I didn't write anything in my journal about this as
it was happening because the whole experience was beyond
words for me--the feelings were too strong. They still
are.

March 3

Alicia seems to be doing fine now--what a relief!
It makes me feel really happy to see her this way again--
I only hope it lasts. I've come to think that it probably won't. I've sort of gotten used to the idea of
expecting another turn for the worst--although as I said
before, I will never be able to accept the thought of
Alicia being in an institution for the rest of her life.
I won't give up the hope that, somehow, something or
someone will make enough difference to her that she will
be able to get herself out of the cycle. I wonder if
everyone else who has ever worked with Alicia has said
the same thing?

March 14

It's been two weeks now and Alicia's still doing
o.k. Had a meeting with Mrs. Kennedy, Dr. Rakosky, and
Mrs. Meredith about Alicia. We've agreed to work together in the same direction for Alicia--sounds hopeful.
Maybe this is what she's needed--several people at once
pushing for the same thing. Mrs. Kennedy really seems to
have had a good effect on Alicia. Alicia seems to really
respect her and be open with her. I'm really grateful to
Mrs. Kennedy for spending the time and effort. She seems
to be a fantastic person--concerned with the patients as
individuals rather than as cases or patients, and one of
the few people in the institution who are like that.
It's too bad there isn't a Mrs. Kennedy for each patient
there--they could all benefit from her. Alicia might
even be going to adult education classes with Mrs.
Kennedy. That would be so good for her. There's also
some talk about her being able to go back to college.
Mrs. Meredith has made an appointment for her to see some
lady. If this comes true it would be a *fantastic* opportunity for her. I hope it's true. This is the chance
she needs--it'll probably be her *only* chance. I really
hope it works out.

March 21

Everything seems to be working out *great*. The adult

education drawing class has started, it's going smoothly,
Alicia had her interview for college, and the prospects
seem pretty good. Alicia is still going strong. It's
been a couple of weeks now--and she still seems to be
doing o.k. Maybe everything will be o.k. from now on--
I guess this is what she needed all this time--a couple
of good people and good things going for her at once.
This will be so great for her. She seems to be really
pleased and so am I. Right now it seems as if nothing
can go wrong. Alicia's even been home a few weekends in
a row and she's still doing fine. Mark and I were at her
house on Friday for a small St. Pat's party which was
really nice and we had a good time. Mrs. Miller was nice
to us too. Alicia's father wasn't home. Alicia was in
her glory playing hostess. She was thoroughly enjoying
herself. *Everything is great!*

March 23

　　Alicia continues to do well--it's really amazing.
She's breaking all her previous records. She seems to be
really psyched for going to college--I keep desperately
hoping that she'll stay this way. Every day that I see
her and she remains this way helps me to believe she's
really going to do it. I guess she's proving it to herself too. I really need to believe she can do it. I
can't believe that life (society, people [?]) could be so
cruel as to force Alicia to be institutionalized her
whole life. But I can also understand how her parents
must feel--unable to handle or really understand her--
wondering why, after all the love they gave her, she is
the way she is. And I can understand why other people
don't want to take risks by hiring or living with her.
I'm not sure whether I could live with her for more than
a year or two without getting either totally discouraged
or totally disgusted. She must feel the same way about
herself at times. So many answers are possible, but none
explains the whole thing. I guess for now I should just
be happy that things are going as well as they are.

April 4

　　Everything is *still* going well--everyone is really

happy about it--especially me! Nothing too much new--
except that Alicia's college bills will probably be paid
by the state which is great because otherwise she might
not be able to go. She doesn't have much money and I
guess she won't take any more from her parents.

I've told her all about the wedding and that she is
invited--she's really excited and looking forward to it
although I'm sure she's also feeling a little sad and en-
vious. She still thinks that I would be a good sister of
St. Joseph. I guess that's because she likes to think
we're very similar and since that's the path she's chosen
(or forced herself into), she'd like someone else to val-
idate her decision and help her think that it's better
that way. By my getting married, I've only added points
to the score of the opposition--but I think she's really
trying to accept it--she knows it's what I want, that
I'll be happy and so will Mark, etc. She is willing to
let me make the decision even if it makes her sad.
That's pretty good because she's usually so adamant about
having her own way.

We're trying to make some plans for spending a day
together--to buy jeans and a denim jacket for Alicia for
school. I think we'll have a really good time. I'm
looking forward to it.

April 18

Well, the disaster I had been hoping against has
happened. I feel that there's not much I can say about
it. I'm really crushed although Mrs. Kennedy doesn't
seem to think that it's so bad. She says that Alicia has
had a lot of things to think about--school, wedding, art
class--and that it probably just seemed overwhelming to
her. I don't know, but I just can't be that optimisitc
at this point. I feel overwhelmed, disappointed, and
down, maybe even a little angry that Alicia would do this
to herself and to me. When I saw her I almost felt like
shaking her and telling her to cut it out and act normal
before she blew her chances--I wondered if she realized
what she was doing to herself and to me. It's hard to
tell whether she does realize it. I really wish she
could understand and *do something* about it. It's almost
impossible at a time like this to treat her with "uncon-

ditional positive regard," but since the opposite reaction is the one I'm sure she's gotten over and over again
(and it hasn't helped that I can see), I'll continue to
try to be positive and encouraging--although it's very
hard for me now. I really wonder if there's any hope,
but I continue to tell myself that there's *got to be*.

April 25

     All of last week was *awful*, Thursday especially--the
bus trip and the rest of my day with Alicia were almost
unbearable. I can accept her the way she is, but I know
others can't and don't and this bothers me. On one hand,
the way she approaches strangers really isn't harmful.
She has fun and she really flips them out, which people
need once in a while. On the other hand, I'm sure she
doesn't win many sympathizers that way--she alienates the
people who she'll have to relate to whether she likes it
or not. It can't be just her way; there has to be some
compromise. I wonder if she realizes how these people
are reacting to her--I realize it and it bothers me. Basically she should be able to be the way she is (since
she isn't hurting anyone) without bad reactions, but I
can see that most people aren't about to let her be this
way. It's taken me a long time to let her be the way she
is and a lot of times I still force her to be my way. So
what should happen? Who should give in? Who will have
to give in? It seems to me that Alicia will have to, but
is that right? Even if it is right, I wonder if she'd
ever be willing to do it.

     Alicia talks a lot about the wedding and still seems
to be looking forward to it.

     It amazes me that, at times, she will talk crazy to
everyone else, but fairly normally to me. She's been
doing this to Dr. Rakosky, Mrs. Kennedy, her mother, the
nurses, and other people in general--but when we're alone
she usually is coherent, calm, and pretty normal. I really wonder why this is. Perhaps she is testing them--or
is she still testing me and how I react when she treats
others this way? In some ways it makes me feel good--
that she can be that way with me. It's nice. It makes
me think that I'm special to her, that she really enjoys
our time together and can be herself with me. I'm glad

she can--I wouldn't want it any other way.

My hope vs. despair battle is still undecided--I guess it will be until there are some signs from Alicia that hope should win.

May 3

Another incident[2]--this time at adult education. Alicia can't really understand (at least that's what she says) why they made her leave--she says it was the teacher who was sick, not her (the teacher was indeed physically sick). I don't know if it would have been better for the teacher and class to have known about Alicia's hospitalization or not--it would have been less trouble the other way, but perhaps it's better for Alicia that it happened this way--but it's really hard to tell.

I hope she'll be allowed to go back. I think it will be a good experience both for her and the class if she has to face them and they her. I also hope Mrs. Kennedy doesn't get in much trouble and that I don't either. It did not seem like we would from what the guy at the desk said last night, but Dr. Rakosky thinks we're in

---

[2] Supplementary note, January, 1974. Alicia had been going to an adult education class in drawing at the local high school. Mrs. Kennedy was taking a class at the same time as Alicia so she drove her to and from class. However, one week Mrs. Kennedy couldn't go, so I drove Alicia to class. I dropped her off and told her I'd be back to pick her up at 10:00. Later, when I got to the school, I couldn't find her, so I went up to her classroom to look for her. I asked some people standing in the room if they knew where she was. Someone said, "I think the police finally came and took her back to the hospital...." I couldn't believe it. I didn't quite know what to do. After questioning several people I got a more complete picture of what had happened. It seems that the drawing teacher had become ill during class and had to leave the room. Alicia decided to take her place and take over the lesson. She started drawing maps on the board, lecturing on Mars, and telling "jokes." People tried to get her to sit down and relax--they thought

big trouble (although he didn't quite have the time to discuss it which makes one really angry).

Alicia should try explaining her jokes (her act in class was all a joke) to people--maybe that would work. I should try to talk to her about it.

She's still constantly talking about the wedding and "What will I do if I _____," with everything from "laugh" to "wet my pants" filling in the blank. I guess she's pretty nervous about it. I try to reassure her, but I don't know if she feels any better about it. She makes it all sound funny and like a joke, but I think she's really concerned about it and doesn't know if she should go or not. I think it'll be really good for her if she can.

May 16

Alicia is doing better now, thank goodness. She's still concerned about getting to and lasting through the wedding, but other than that she seems back on her way toward a normal period. I wonder how long this one will last? I hope that if she does make it to the wedding that everything goes well. She's talked and worried

---

she was having a nervous breakdown on the spot. Eventually, the night school supervisor was called in and he tried to contact her "home," but reached the state hospital. No one at the school knew Alicia was from the hospital. We had decided that it would be best for Alicia if no one knew that she was "different" in any way and when her enrollment card asked for a number to call in case of an emergency, the hospital number was given, as if it were her home phone number. The night superintendent sent the police over to pick Alicia up and bring her back to the hospital. I drove to the hospital as quickly as possible because I knew that none of the night staff really knew about the arrangements which had been made for Alicia to go to school, the transportation which had been arranged, etc. They wouldn't let me see Alicia--they said she was quite upset. I was questioned by the night superintendent and was asked to leave.

Alicia never did go back to her class.

about it so much that I'm beginning to get scared and to
believe that maybe things won't work out o.k. for her at
the wedding. I really hope that they do--I don't know
how I'll manage if they don't. I just wonder if she'll
be able to handle all the people, the excitement, etc.
I guess we'll see soon enough.

It's hard to believe the year is over. I'm glad I
don't have to stop seeing Alicia. I'd always be so curi-
ous as to what was happening with her. It would be really hard to say good-bye. I wonder, though, whether anything has been accomplished. I know a friendship has
been formed, but I really wonder if that's enough to
change anything. It's so hard to see if any change has
happened in a person, other than behavioral change, but
that's not always the most important kind.

I know that I've gained a lot from the experience,
but it would make it much more complete if Alicia has
gained something, too. I guess whatever has happened has
been a good thing for both of us. At least each of us is
that much closer to another human being.

ALICIA MILLER

FOLLOW-UP INTERVIEW

Oh Paul, you came all the way from Switzerland to see me!

JP - Don't get nervous. I just want to talk with you about the student program here at the hospital. I believe you had a student.

You mean Karen. You bet we're going to talk. You know I want to take a couple of collie dogs with us to Saturn....I suggest Tide to clean the whole place. Really filthy here.

JP - You're talking crazy....At least in a way that I can't follow you.

Yeah. I'm talking in poetry.

JP - What did you think of the students coming here?

I loved the students coming here. This is a great place, but the bathrooms really need cleaning.

JP - You used to talk like this with Karen?

One day I mentioned to her she might have twelve kids. She has a husband.... Each have a car....She has a bus, and he has a small car....Enough for twelve kids. What do you want to know for?

JP - I'm trying to understand and learn more about the effects of the student program, especially how the patients see them. I'm having a hard time with you, though.

That's true--I don't know what to say. I talk in poetry and you talk in poetry. The program is very good, but I won't need it when I get to Saturn--I'm ready to leave April 2nd and come back June 7th....When you talk to me, it's like I'm talking to Karen....Can't I preserve a little bit of innocence?

JP - I'm still interested in your impressions of Karen.

> I've got a tummyache--got to leave to go to the bathroom. Will you be able to rest here for a few minutes, Doctor?

JP - Will you be back?

> Yes.

(Interruption)

> I did have to take a tiny leak.

JP - You have a student assigned to you now?

> Yes. Karen. At least as far as I know.

JP - When was the last time you saw her?

> Let's see, today is Tuesday. Must have been last Thursday.

JP - I see. She's been coming this year as well as last?

> This is 1973, isn't it?

JP - What do you and Karen talk about?

> Don't you realize that I get tired of talking (sad)....The problem is my fa-ther....My father is Teddy Kennedy.... Do you find me pretty?...Boy, you're handsome....You must be Carol's hus-band....How about examining me! (Point-ing to a nearby bed)

JP - No. I just want to talk with you.

> (Silence)

JP - Ever get help from Karen?

> (Silence)

JP - Is it painful for you to talk about her?

> Yes. (Nodding her head, then singing quietly) When you see Karen coming down the street...She graduated magna cum laude. She wants to be a doctor, too....I can't have her manning the

controls when I go to Saturn--jeepers-creepers. I'll see space and never get back.

JP - How long have you been in the hospital?

Too long!

JP - How many years?

Nine years.

JP - What caused you to come here?

May I cry for a minute?

JP - Sure.

(Alicia cries quietly)

JP - You are a very sad girl.

Not really. I want to ski in the Olympics. I'd love to ski nude in Colorado. I'll do it nude for my country....I love what John Kennedy said....Ask not what your country can do for you.

JP - I guess you don't want to talk about Karen?

You mean are we going to talk about what you want to talk about or what I want to talk about.

JP - Yes.

Karen doesn't know what to talk about. She says "what?"--I say "what?" We're like two ducks....Her husband is beautiful though....I don't know what to say....I love Johnny MacDonald....He's a priest....Am I getting a proposal?

JP - Not from me. I'm only here to inquire about the student program.

Karen is a walking saint, too. No kidding, she's a "walking saint."

JP - Do you really believe that?

I know that! Boy, this place is filthy!...I really need to clean it up. (Pause)

> I get it. This interview is kind of like research. You know Karen is four months pregnant.

JP - When did she tell you that?

> She didn't have to tell me. I can see it. I'm the Einstein kid.

JP - Are you pregnant?

> No. What made you ask that?

JP - Well, you're kind of fat.

> Hee hee. Will you excuse me for a minute (thirty seconds pause). I saw a fawn under the apple tree.

JP - Is this Karen's first baby?

> Yes. She wants to do it natural. I bet she's going to have twelve children. I can't tell her that anymore. It'll make her sick--thinking of having twelve children.

JP - Did you ask her if she's pregnant?

> I know she is by the way she walks.... She's liable to unload right away.... We're both talking in poetry.

JP - Do you want to talk straight?

> Certainly.

JP - You don't scare her?

> I hope not.

JP - You scare me a bit.

> Thanks for telling me.

JP - I don't know quite what to do....With the moving from topic to topic kind of thing. Do you mean to scare people?

> You're hurting me. I'm trying to do my best to protect you....I'll tell you why this hospital didn't pass the cleanliness inspection.

JP - I'm not inspecting the hospital.

> Karen and I are in trouble....You know what my idea is for an insurance company?...I really respect Mutual of Omaha and they're in a lot of trouble. (Pause)
> Karen's going to have twin boys....Two boys....I know!

JP - Do I scare you?

> Yes. You're asking me lots of questions. (Sadly) Really petrified! (Laughing) I wish I had read "Profiles in Courage." I am getting amnesia.... Do you believe in "Free Will"?

JP - You mean she can come or not come?

> She can come and go as she pleases. She's puffed up like anything--puff, puff, puff. She's still at the university this year. She said that she's going to try to come as much as she can. I think she feels sorry for me. But she shouldn't. I like it here. I don't want to leave the hospital, except in the Space Program.

JP - Do you like her to feel sorry for you?

> Oh, that poor girl. I know she has empathy for me, but I don't want followers....Who wants followers when you're doing cancer research?...I'm trying to protect you. You're innocent. I've died a couple of times. Heaven is a crowded place.

JP - Do you want Karen to keep coming?

> When I was at her house....I don't know what to do with my mother....She brought me cookies and apples, etc.

JP - Do people do too much for you?

> She's like a daughter to me....I'm afraid she will lose her children if

she talks to me.

JP - You're pretty powerful, huh?

(Nodding yes) I hope she doesn't
though. She brings gifts to me and I
give gifts to her. Then she goes out
in the sunshine.

JP - You really like Karen?

I sure do!

JP - What in particular?

She's a good friend of mine. I have
pictures of us together at the wedding.
Invited me to her wedding. Got me
these expensive shoes and a dress. Yes,
I went to the wedding in New Jersey.
For a moment, she did not want me to go
though. I was really scared, I think,
getting on that plane, going to the wedding....She's going to have twins in
August, you know.

JP - Was Karen scared at her wedding?

It was really crowded there. I spread
out a blue mantle for her.

JP - How did you get back here?

I came back in a plane. My parents
came to the airport and picked up
Patricia Nelson and me. I'm scared of
my mother--that's why I can't go home.
(Crying) Are they going to replace
what they did to me in the infirmary?
They gave me a complete hysterectomy.
I can't have any children ever. I was
raped. Not really. I really don't
know if that's true or not.

JP - When did that happen?

Last year. Actually, I don't think it
happened at all.

JP - Oh, by the way, I know Pat. She was one of
the students I supervised in another course.

Is she red-headed?

Yes, that's her.

JP - I bet she watched you like a hawk on the
trip and at the wedding.

Yes. She's a sister of the Immaculate
Conception. Pat is a good friend of
Karen's. Pat is in Canton, Ohio.
Praying for you. Karen is beautiful
and Pat is beautiful.

JP - Do you think either of them will end up
here in the hospital? Like as a patient?

I don't want them to. Because this
hospital is full. You consider me
sick?

JP - Yes. Because you won't talk straight.
It's hard to have a conversation with you.

That's true.

JP - It's interesting that you seem afraid of
Mother, but not Pat or Karen.

I'm not afraid of you either. About
thirty-two minutes ago I was. I
thought you were out to get me. Does
the press want to come up here and take
pictures?

JP - Are those questions about my taking notes
of this conversation?

How would you like to walk out of this
hospital with just a pen and nothing
else? I'm sorry. I have an active
imagination.

JP - Why are you afraid of Mother? Is it because she gives you too much--grapes, ap-
ples, cookies? Then makes you feel guilty?

Yes. (Sadly) I want real lemons and
not the stuff in the cafeteria.

JP - Got problems with Mother?

I sure do.

JP - What about your father?

> He's sorry he didn't allow me any tel-
> ephone calls. The student program is
> excellent. It's probably sad for you
> to see them go. You're a good teacher.

JP - Yes. Is it sad for you too?

> Yes. It's sad to see the students
> graduate. All of them. Sammy Allport
> was in my class. He figured out how to
> make the space vehicle go. One cup of
> flour, one cup of oil, and Vaseline....

JP - Who has it better in life--you or Karen?

> I feel a little bit sorry for Karen.
> Well, she wants to be a mother and I
> don't want her to lose her children.
> She's in love with her husband.

JP - Is she having trouble with her pregnancy?

> I hope she doesn't. Karen comes as of-
> ten as she can. I know she shouldn't
> come too often, because the hospital
> isn't that clean.

JP - What would you do if you had one wish?

> Oh brother! I told you I was a nun.
> I don't want to leave my vows.

JP - And you really did keep quiet at the wedding, huh?

> Yes. But I was dressed up too much.
> I had a hysterectomy in the infirmary.
> Not really, I took too much soap, and
> they had to clean out my stomach.

JP - Were you pregnant?

> Yes. I went into the bathroom and they
> got me angry. So I ate the soap. They
> were nurses and kept giving me needles.
> I heard all this music and saw the
> cross. Oh, believe me, I really saw
> the cross. Our trouble is that we wear
> shoes in this hospital, and when we go

home, we bring the dirt home.   That's
our trouble.

JP - Well, I guess we better stop.   Thanks for
talking with me.

5

MERTHIOLATE WAS APPLIED

Debby and Ruth

When Debbie asks Ruth what she thinks about as she sits on the ward, day after day, rocking back and forth, she learns, "Saturdays she thinks about her sister coming to visit and Thursdays she thinks about me coming to visit and the rest of the time she doesn't think about anything."

So many of our own reveries involve thinking about real and imagined interactions with other people in our lives. Is the need of the mental patient for emotional, sustaining human interaction different from the need we experience? The institutions which house patients are often described as depersonalizing because of their regimentation and lack of privacy. What happens when memory alone performs the task of defining oneself, a function usually served by ongoing relationships? If reverie is so changed that thoughts about people slow down and acquire sameness from day to day, then depersonalization has a deeper, more profound meaning.

By recognizing the importance of human relationships to reality testing, self-definition, and growth, and by recognizing the hope that one close relationship may encourage an isolated person to try other new relationships, student-companion programs are motivated. Ruth had been institutionalized for twenty-three years, and Debby's repeated question was, "How can I help her?" Debby liked Ruth, and offered her a relationship the limits of which

Debby freely acknowledged. In response to Ruth's extended isolation and dependence, and in recognition of
her own limited commitment, Debby took Ruth out, encour-
aged her to build a relationship with another patient,
tried to help her secure a job, and tried to impress the
staff with Ruth's value as a person. Also, Debby used
her fondness for and acceptance of Ruth in trying to
raise Ruth's self-esteem. At year's end, Debby was
frank, both about leaving and about Ruth's importance to
her.

Ruth's interview, filled with themes of isolation
and the need for human interaction, is perhaps the most
moving document of the book. At first, Ruth seemed in-
different and said she didn't remember Debby's name.
Later, her real feelings about Debby became apparent and
they illustrate how people remain isolated despite their
need for human contact.

As you read Debby's diary and Ruth's interview, consider the human need for interpersonal relationships in
which to grow and define the self. All of the patients
in this book share a common lack of human companionship.
"This is a hospital for the insane," Ruth tells us.
"They brought me here and I stay here."

BETHLEHEM STATE HOSPITAL

MEDICAL RECORD

Ruth Stevens   Patient #58039

ADMISSION NOTE - MARCH 3, 1948

This is a thirty-year-old white female, admitted because she was depressed, worried, excited, and at times abusive. Also, she had
threatened to set fire to a neighbor's house and
she had exposed herself. A review of the etiological factors reveals that patient is one of
ten siblings born to a mentally deficient mother
who had a history of several admissions to this
hospital, and a father who was alcoholic, abusive to the family, and who otherwise conducted
himself in a psychopathic manner. The mother's
diagnosis on each of her three admissions was
the same--psychosis with mental deficiency, I.Q.
51. The father has not provided for the family
for a number of years and he apparently has little to do with them. Despite the acknowledged
handicaps, the patient, through her own efforts
and the efforts of the Society for the Prevention of Cruelty to Children, completed her high
school education at the age of twenty-one. It
appears that the patient was getting along fairly satisfactorily in life until she suffered
what she referred to as a nervous breakdown in
1943. It lasted a month during which time she
was cared for by her sister. The next crucial
incident in her life was a pregnancy resulting
from her promiscuity with her first lover. This
man allegedly went to California when he learned
of her pregnancy. Since that time there has
been a gradual withdrawal from social contacts,
with increasing seclusiveness and the development of ideas of reference toward strangers.
She was withdrawn entirely from church activity.
Her immoral conduct has persisted with a tendency towards overindulgence and a growing un-
concern regarding morals and ethics of such behavior. The reasons for her commitment are not

166

too well founded. Allegedly, she threatened to
burn the house down and had been exposing herself. These complaints, as far as can be determined, were registered by a woman who is now
deceased and, therefore, is unavailable for cir-
cumstantiation of these charges.

MENTAL SUMMARY - MARCH 15, 1948

GENERAL APPEARANCE   Patient is a well-developed,
slightly obese thirty-year-old single woman. She
is slovenly in appearance and has not attempted
to make herself attractive since being in the
hospital. Her facial expressions are usually appropriate for the occasion. She smiles readily,
scowls when angry, but appears quite perplexed
at times.

ATTITUDE   Her attitude when she entered the hospital was that of rebellion and resulted in her
attempted flight. During the first week of her
hospital stay, her attitude was one of indifference with overtones of perplexity. She did not
want to talk with the examiner and continually
expressed the idea that it was up to the hospital
staff to prove that she was insane, but at the
same time, she admitted that perhaps she was
mentally ill.

DIAGNOSTIC IMPRESSIONS   Present mental status
examination reveals severely impaired insight
and judgment, shallow affectivity, no frank delusions or hallucinations. About the only evidence of psychosis at this time is her shallow
affect, ideas of reference, tendency to seclusiveness, and withdrawal from environment.

        The examiner offers the diagnosis of
Schizophrenia, Simple Type.

MARCH 20, 1948   The patient was finally persuaded to have a gynecological examination. Before the examination she commandeered a wheel
chair and rode up and down the corridor with a
child-like smile on her face. When asked if she
was enjoying herself, she replied that she wasn't

<u>playing</u>, she just wanted to know how it worked.
She shows little insight into her condition....

APRIL 24, 1948   Visit. Condition: Improved.
Patient is well enough to try visiting her home.
She is not to live with her feeble-minded mother.
To report to clinic.

JULY 17, 1948   Mrs. Heard of the Department of
Public Welfare telephoned this date to report
that the patient is at the local hospital with
pains. She is evidently pregnant. The patient
did not stay with her sister following her release on visit. Instead, she has been keeping
house for Mr. Ballou. Recently the patient has
been looking for a man or men. As soon as the
patient's pains are gone she will be returned to
Bethlehem State Hospital.

OCTOBER 24, 1948   Returned from visit by police.
Was brought to police station yesterday for ne-
glect of children. Was very noisy and destructive in jail last night. Admitted to in-patient
status.

APRIL 21, 1949   Absence. Condition: Improved
(custody of sister). Home for the weekend.[1]

MARCH 5, 1951   The patient is an overweight
young woman who has very good coloring. She believes she is crucified because her food is
tasteless. Many of her answers are inappropriate and she laughs when answering almost every
question. She expresses a desire to see her
youngest child and have her know that she is her
mother. It is possible that she is hallucinated.

OCTOBER 18, 1951   A copy of a citation was
served on this patient today by Sheriff Cole in
regard to the adoption of the patient's son.

---

[1] In the subsequent two years, there were ten weekend
absences, in care of sister, each noted without comment.

ANNUAL NOTE - MARCH 6, 1954

Patient resides on Ward Three. She is
fairly tidy but not interested in her personal
appearance. She is cooperative, does no work,
and is not assaultive or destructive, but she is
inactive. Patient expresses no delusions but
she hardly talks at all, just grins, is idle,
and picks her skin constantly. Memory is fair,
judgment impaired; patient has no insight. She
eats and sleeps well and expresses no physical
complaints. Patient was on Equanil. There was
no appreciable change and so it was discontinued.

OCTOBER 5, 1954   Transferred from Ward Three.
Patient is catatonic--displays typical waxy flexibility. Cannot walk to the cafeteria. Patient
was prepared for ECT. She was placed on Ritalin.

No improvement.

NOVEMBER 6, 1954   Absence. Condition: Improved.
Custody of sister. Improved on ECT. Well enough
for a weekend visit only.

ANNUAL NOTE - FEBRUARY 11, 1958

Patient was seen today on Ward Three. The
patient is not cooperative, neat, tidy, or interested in her personal appearance. She assists
with nothing. She is assaultive, destructive,
and does not mingle with others or partake in
any of the ward activities. She expresses no delusions, but is hallucinated in the auditory
sphere; she talks to the walls and to herself.
She is withdrawn, but likes to pull hair. She is
oriented in all three spheres. Her memory is bad
for recent and remote events and her judgment is
impaired. She has no insight into her condition.
She eats well, sleeps soundly, and expresses no
complaints. She looks very tired and listless.
Medication is Thorazine.

MARCH 15, 1958   Transferred--patient has been

restless for a few weeks and hallucinating.
Yesterday she suddenly became violent, tried to
choke some other patient, and was threatening to
kill herself. She no longer is suited for parole. She is on Stelazine, Serpasil, Artane,
and Thorazine.

REPORT OF ACCIDENT AND INJURY - APRIL 6, 1958

        The above-named patient put her fist
through a window. Patient has a cut on the
first finger of her right hand, also her thumb.
Areas were cleansed with soap and water and
painted with tincture of merthiolate.

APRIL 25, 1958   Group Therapy. Attended five
of the eleven Group Therapy sessions held in
March. Patient attributed her absences to a
severe case of athlete's foot. She continued to
be silent and vaguely responsive.[2]

MARCH 1, 1961   Transferred. Has regressed.
Sits and rocks in chair. Agitated. Asked to
come back to Ward Three because she was getting
too nervous. Feared she would become assaultive. Pushed a window out on Ward Three as soon
as she came over here.

REPORT OF ACCIDENT AND INJURY - OCTOBER 5, 1961
Patient put her hand through a pane of glass.
Superficial lacerations on three fingers. Mer-
thiolate was applied.

JULY 2, 1962   Patient was found breaking windows with a chair on the day hall. She did not
receive any injury.

SEPTEMBER 14, 1962   Patient broke two windows

---

[2]Subsequent entries note that Ruth attended two sessions in May, three in June, two in July, five in August,
four in September, four in October, and one in November.
She is reported as sitting quietly in the group.

in the water section with her right hand. Patient has small cuts. Painted with merthiolate.

REPORT OF ACCIDENT AND INJURY - APRIL 22, 1963
Patient broke two panes of glass on the day
hall, causing two small cuts on her right hand
each measuring 0.5-1.0 cm. in length.

REPORT OF ACCIDENT AND INJURY - MAY 21, 1963
For no apparent reason, the patient threw a
chair at the window, breaking three panes of
glass....

REPORT OF ACCIDENT AND INJURY - MAY 23, 1963
Patient broke two panes of glass in the day
hall, cutting the fourth finger on her right
hand....

MARCH 6, 1964   Transferred (to another ward).
Patient has improved and wants to learn the
laundry business. Chance will be given to her.

MAY 18, 1964   Transferred. Breaking windows
and mirrors. Hostile, uncontrollable. Needs
supervision.

MAY 3, 1965   Patient has a small, superficial
scarification on right side of her face sus-
tained when she attacked another patient for
calling her vile names.

MAY 5, 1965   The patient knocked Bertha Wisocki
to the floor. No pathology found.

MAY 7, 1965   The patient pulled Lillian Briggs
to the floor by her hair. No bruises or inju-
ries noted. Ruth was placed in seclusion after
breaking six windows.

AUGUST 12, 1965   Patient kicked patient Olga
Miller while in the cafeteria. She also slapped
her across the face....

OCTOBER 5, 1965   Patient struck another patient, Martha Buss, with such force that she
fell to the floor, landing on her right side....

APRIL 23, 1966   Absence. Condition unimproved,
care of sister. Patient wants to go with her
sister and I think this will be good for her.[3]

OCTOBER 20, 1969   Patient is an overweight woman who is always very clean but usually somewhat sloppy. She spends her time sewing. Suddenly, for no reason, she will get up, take a
chair or a book and break several windows, then
return to her sewing as though nothing had happened. Whenever she sits in a chair, she rocks
back and forth constantly. The motive for her
window breaking seems to be her desire to be put
in seclusion so she can masturbate. Sometimes
it is sufficient to allow her to rest in her
room, but other times she will continue to break
windows until she achieves seclusion. She very
seldom speaks and only in the past month has
carried on any conversations with me. She is
visited at least weekly by her sister who takes
her out for the day. The sister built a home
for Ruth and her mother at one time when Ruth
stayed with her for a year. Ruth could have
this home and live in it if she wished or have
a live-in companion. She tells me that she is
thinking about it. Present medication is
Stelazine, Artane, and Thorazine. During the
past year, no medication that she has been on
seems to have any effect whatsoever on her window breaking.

JULY 6, 1970   Returned from visit by brother.
Patient has broken windows at home because she
wasn't sleeping and was bothered by noises from
the furnace. Voices in the television bothered
her too. They were saying things particularly
to her. Affect is blunt. She is withdrawn and

---

[3]During the subsequent two years, numerous visits to
Ruth's sister are noted in the chart.

keeps rocking during the interview because there
is nothing to do while she is sitting.   She is
on Thorazine.

ANNUAL NOTE - SEPTEMBER 5, 1970

     Patient is on a regular commitment, Section
82.   She has been here since age of thirty.   Her
sister has regularly taken the patient home on
visit but apparently is not interested in taking
the patient on an indefinite visit.   Therefore,
there are plans for the patient to go to a rest
home.

DEBBY'S BETHLEHEM DIARY

October 6

My first meeting with Ruth Stevens was a pleasant one. We had little trouble talking, considering we did not know each other. Ruth seems to be a normal, slightly overweight, fifty-three-year-old woman. We talked mostly about neutral things and took a walk. Ruth said she has a sister who visits and a brother. I was discouraged to learn that she has been in the hospital for twenty-three years--since she was thirty years old. She said she was out for a year some years ago but came back because her sister couldn't stand her any longer.

October 13

Ruth was very talkative today. I can see now why she isn't just a normal lady in her fifties. I don't know what to believe, but Ruth said when she was twenty-one she got a ride home on a snowy day with two men and nothing happened but she felt she was pregnant. The doctors brought her to the hospital where she said she was having a baby although she wasn't. She does have a daughter, she says, who is twenty-two and lives in Texas. The daughter's in her third pregnancy and Ruth says she lived a year with her daughter while she was pregnant. Ruth kept vomiting--she was carrying the baby. Poor Ruth, I guess her sexual upbringing was pretty bad and she wants to be a mother. Ruth also breaks windows when she "is sick" (her words).

I'm learning more about her but I don't know how I can help her.

October 20

Today Ruth and I went for a walk and then to the canteen. We decided next week to make a Halloween trick-or-treat bag for her niece, Pat. I talked to Ruth about going to the OT room during the week but she wasn't very enthusiastic. Edna, her sister, took Ruth out on Saturday as she does every Saturday.

October 27

Ruth and I made Halloween things today with Louise and Helen. They seemed to enjoy it. Helen is even more passive than Ruth but Ruth's so agreeable I don't know what she'd like to do. After twenty-three years of being hospitalized she's probably learned that being agreeable and doing what people tell you to do is the best way to get along without any hassles.

We didn't have much time to talk today. Next week we'll go for a walk and get a chance to talk more. When I left Ruth, I felt as though something was missing. I felt as though I let her down in some way by not having a quiet talk between the two of us. We may not have had much to say but I think she should have someone to listen to her in case there's something she wants to talk about.

November 3

Ruth and I went for a walk outside today and Ruth said the doctor checked her over this week. The doctor asked if she was having a baby and she said she had one already. I've got to find out if she really has a daughter.

I'd like to get Ruth to do things on her own. She really likes to go out; since she knows her way around so well I told her maybe I could try to get ground privileges so she could go out by herself during the week. Ruth said she wouldn't want to go by herself. She really clings to the security of a locked ward. I don't know how I can get her to want to go out by herself. I think it will be very hard to make any progress with Ruth but at least she enjoys my visits.

November 10

I went to see Mrs. Olsen, the head nurse, to ask her about Ruth but she didn't know much. I'm going to see her again in two weeks. I didn't have too much time to spend with Ruth after seeing Mrs. Olsen but we went for a walk. We didn't have much to talk about anyway. We had a Coke and she seemed rather anxious when some attendants

sat near us. We left when they came. We planned to go
shopping next week and have lunch out.

November 17

    We couldn't go shopping today because Louise, another
student in the program, had to study and we were going to
have her and Helen, Louise's patient, come with us.
Louise and I called to tell Ruth and Helen we wouldn't be
early but to expect us at the regular time. Ruth was a
little disappointed that we didn't get to go downtown but
I said I'd be sure to take her some time. We did go for
a long walk down the street, looked in the store windows,
and had Cokes and bagels in a luncheonette. It was a
good day. Ruth told me all about life before she went to
Bethlehem. Her mother went to the state hospital when
Ruth was seventeen so she lived with her father awhile.
Her sisters left to attend school and live elsewhere.
Ruth's father left (who knows where he went) and Ruth
lived with a lady in a boarding house. Then she lived
here and there and had different jobs. When she was in
her twenties she lived with her mother who got out of the
hospital and then Ruth went into Bethlehem. It must have
been really rough for her when she was young. Screaming
mother, poor, left alone at seventeen. No wonder she
can't cope with life and would rather stay at Bethlehem.
I really like old Ruth. I hope I can do something for
her. I told her I liked to visit her and she was glad to
hear it. I talked to her about moving up a ward and
working and she'd like to try it. It will be hard for
her but I think she can handle a job outside the hospital.
I think she'd enjoy it. I'm really going to push for
privileges and a better ward for Ruth.

November 24

    Ruth and I went out for a little while today but it
was cold so we only went to the canteen for awhile. When
we were getting ready to go out I noticed something I
didn't like too much. Another woman in the hospital was
going out also and about four or five attendants were
fussing over her, getting her a coat that looked good and
making sure she was warm. Meanwhile, Ruth's standing

there and no one seems to care if she has gloves or a hat
or if her legs will be cold and I felt bad for Ruth. I
wonder if she feels neglected when she sees other people
being taken care of while she is ignored. She must have
noticed it unless she's so used to it that she expects
that kind of treatment. I should have done something to
make sure that the attendants would realize Ruth needed
gloves too, but instead I asked her to wear mine.

Helen was moved back a ward today. It kind of depressed me because I feel our hour visits don't really
interfere very much with institutional life. Poor Helen
was really shaken up by it but maybe it will motivate her
to take better care of herself (that is, do what the
nurses and attendants expect). I asked Ruth to try to
help Helen be comfortable when she comes on the ward.
I'd really like to see them work together to help each
other while we, the students, are gone. The problem is
neither one of them has much initiative so I don't know
if it will work.

December 1

Ruth went home for four days over Thanksgiving. She
left last Wednesday when I was there and I met her sister.
Her sister said Ruth and she were both strong-willed and
they didn't get along too well when they lived together
for a year. It seemed strange talking about Ruth while
she was standing there. I don't know if she felt strange.

When Ruth was back at the hospital Monday she was put
onto Ward Three for awhile. She told me she didn't feel
good so they put her there. She didn't know exactly what
was wrong with herself.

I spoke to a nurse, Miss Larson, and she said Ruth
was very nervous Monday. She was rocking back and forth
very fast, much faster than her usual rocking. She didn't
know if Ruth was upset about being back at the hospital or
about having been at her sister's house. Ruth asked to be
put on Ward Three so they brought her there and let her
lie down. Later Ruth came out and said she felt like
breaking windows so they locked her in the room. By sup-
pertime she was all right and she seemed o.k., although a
little nervous, when I talked to her today.

Ruth didn't know what was wrong with herself Monday
or she couldn't tell me. I still think Ruth is basically
all right, even though occasionally she feels like breaking windows. I still don't know how much I can help her.
I wish I had more time to see her and also to talk to the
staff. She's been there twenty-three years so everyone
probably figures there's no hope for her and they've
stopped trying. I guess I should try to get the idea
across to the staff that Ruth has about twenty years of
her life left and she shouldn't spend them locked up,
sitting and rocking all day long on Ward Two.

December 8

Today was a pretty good day. Ruth, Louise, and I
went downtown, looked in stores, and ate lunch out. I
got a chance to see the hospital routine a little earlier
and later than I usually do. The ward's a lot different
after lunch when a lot of the patients go to sleep because their bedrooms are unlocked. Ruth doesn't sleep
during the day but stays awake rocking in her chair.

Helen was supposed to come downtown with us but she
didn't want to. We tried to talk her into it for fifteen
minutes but she wouldn't come. She's really pretty badly
off. She doesn't like Ward Two, but she won't do anything
to get off it. Louise is getting really frustrated.

Being downtown was like any other day, shopping and
eating out. I wasn't anxious at all about being with
Ruth and I don't think anyone else noticed anything
strange about her. A lot of old people dress rather poorly so people probably thought she was a poor older woman
if they thought anything of her at all. Ruth is really
so normal (at least most of the time). People expect little from her and get little, I think. She's capable of
much more than is expected of her.

One good thing I found out today is that the attendants (or at least one attendant) feel that Ruth is more
talkative now than she used to be. I was talking to one
of them (should have gotten her name) and told her how
well Ruth was getting along. She enjoys going out, is
pleasant. She's talkative, considering she doesn't have
much new to say, and I really enjoy visiting her. I hope

the rest of the staff will begin to look upon Ruth a little differently than they have.

December 15

It was very cold today so we didn't go out. The
ward was looking very Christmasy and Ruth said she helped
put up some of the decorations. We went down to the canteen and had a Coke. There was no place to sit so we sat
in the library but the man who works there told us there
was no eating or drinking allowed. He was very nice in
telling us, though, and Ruth and I both agreed he seemed
like a kind man. Ruth said he reminded her of an old
boyfriend but she didn't go into it. When we got back to
Ward Two we played checkers awhile and looked around the
ward at the Christmas decorations.

When Ruth was sitting in her regular chair in the
hall I asked her what she thinks about all day as she
rocks. She said Saturdays she thinks about her sister
coming to visit and Thursdays she thinks about me coming
to visit and the rest of the time she doesn't think
about anything. I almost believe that she sits there
without daydreaming or thinking of anything unless some
motion on the floor interrupts her rocking.

Again I was talking to Ruth about privileges but she
doesn't think she's ready for them. There's something
terribly wrong with an institution that makes a fifty-
three-year-old woman believe that she really needs to be
locked up, that she can't be responsible for any of her
actions.

For twenty-three years she's been locked up and
supervised and she can't imagine doing things on her
own. Whatever problems brought Ruth to the hospital
when she was young were small, I'm sure, compared to
her present problem of complete dependence and acceptance of institutional life. I tell her she can do
things on her own but no one has been telling her that
for the past twenty-three years. All she can do is
maker her bed, take her medicine, eat, and sleep when
they tell her to. I've seen her outside and inside the
hospital and I'm sure she's capable of much more--if
only she will believe she is.

December 22

Today was the last day I'd see Ruth before Christmas. She seemed in pretty good spirits and told me she's going home for four days. I brought her a Christmas present which I think she liked. The hospital also gave her some things and a sweater for her to give her sister. I guess there is some money in a fund for her but I don't know where it's from.

Ruth got a Christmas card from her daughter. I wish I knew more about her daughter but I haven't had time yet to speak to anyone about it.

We stayed on the ward today. I think Ruth was afraid her sister would come for her while she was out. Ruth asked me if I wanted to play ping-pong so we played awhile and then another patient played with Ruth.

I don't know if it's the Christmas season or a change in Ruth but the attendants (at least two more) seemed to pay her more attention than usual. One attendant who has been working on Ward Two for less than a month seems to be very nice to Ruth. I wish Ruth wanted some privileges because now would be a good time to ask for them.

Ruth knows I won't see her for a week or two and although I think she'll miss my visits, I think she'll manage without me. Maybe I'll send her a letter or two while I'm at home.

February 3

I've seen Ruth quite a few times since the last time I wrote in this book. I visited her during finals and she had been moved to Ward One from Ward Two. I saw her in the afternoon and she was watching the soap operas on T.V. It was a nice day but she didn't want to go out because she had already been outside for a walk with one of the other patients.

I couldn't believe it. She really went out with just another patient and no guardian. She said before that she wasn't ready and didn't want to go out, but when given the opportunity she did. I'm glad someone moved her up and gave her ground privileges. Ruth even went

down to the canteen by herself. Before this, she didn't
want to go anywhere alone.

I left feeling really happy that Ruth had moved up
to One. Maybe in some way I helped Ruth by bringing her
to the attention of some staff members. Ruth was ready
for a change a long time ago but no one took any notice
of her because she's so agreeable.

I was a little worried that I wouldn't be able to
find things for us to do if Ruth was going out a lot with
other people and wouldn't be wanting to go out when I
came, but, overall, I was happy for her.

Now that I look back on it, I was being as ridiculous
as the hospital staff. I considered moving up a ward to
be a great achievement but just because the hospital staff
puts a patient on another ward, it doesn't cure all the
patient's problems. But at least, by moving her up a
ward, the staff seemed to take more interest in Ruth and
perhaps they'll expect more of her and get it.

When I went back the next week, Ruth was on Two.
She was still sleeping on One but spending her days on
Two. Whether this was a regression or whether or not it
makes much difference what ward a patient is on, I don't
know. I don't think Ruth will ask the attendants to open
the door for her so she probably won't be using her ground
privileges.

Ruth and I went to the canteen and played checkers on
the open ward. The next week I visited her we played
cards on the open ward. I think I should try to keep our
activities off the locked ward and on the open ward, if
not off hospital grounds. When we played cards a male
friend of mine played also. Ruth is a little afraid of
men but she seemed to relax and enjoy the game after a few
minutes of being around Ted. I think it was good for her
to interact with a man for a change.

February 11

Ruth was in a very good mood when I came to see her
today. She had on a new dress she had just received and
was happy about it. She was washing out an old dress on
Ward One when I got there. We talked for awhile on the

ward. She didn't go home the last weekend so she hadn't
been out in awhile. It was too cold for us to go out so
we walked around the hospital, ending up at the music
room on the third floor. There were a few stereos up
there and a cabinet full of records. A music teacher was
there with one of the women patients who was practicing
her piano lesson. She had been taking lessons for only
six months and she was doing well. The music teacher,
thinking I was a patient, asked me if I wanted to take
piano lessons. I didn't tell him I wasn't a patient but
told him I couldn't take lessons. Ruth wasn't very interested in piano lessons either. We played an album for
awhile and left.

Later on we went to the canteen and then played
rummy on the open ward. Lately we seem to be playing
checkers and cards more often than talking. Maybe I've
known Ruth long enough to have heard most of her life experiences outside the hospital. Her life inside the hospital has been dull and monotonous so she has little to
say about that. Friday we start cooking classes on Two
so maybe Ruth's life will be a bit more exciting.

February 18

Ruth's been offered a job. The nurses on Two asked
her if she would like to work in the kitchen at the infirmary. Ruth was not too thrilled about the idea. She
really doesn't want any responsibility but she may take
the job.

She and I walked over to the infirmary building to
take a look at the kitchen. When we walked in, there
was a group of employees sitting around talking. I asked
them where the kitchen was and Ruth and I walked down to
it. Ruth wanted to turn back with every step we took but
I assured her there was nothing to be nervous about.

We found another group of employees sitting around
outside the kitchen. I looked at the kitchen and asked
Ruth to come down to look at it. Ruth didn't want to and
I had to put my hand on her shoulder and lead her to the
kitchen to assure her there was nothing to fear.

The woman in there talked to us and I asked her if
they needed help in the kitchen. She thought I was going

to work until I told her it was Ruth. Often you really
can't tell the patients from the visitors. The woman was
nice and said she really could use someone. Ruth was
nervous and looked pained. When we left Ruth said she
may try it. She was concerned that she would be the only
patient working in the kitchen. Before this, I thought
she was more afraid of the other patients than of employees and visitors but I guess she gets nervous over everyone new.

We went and got something to drink and came back to
the ward.

The job Ruth was offered may be pretty bad but it
might help her. I don't think she'll get paid though,
because they pay in cigarettes and she doesn't smoke.
I hope she can handle it. She hasn't had any responsibility for a long time.

February 25

Ruth seems to be more nervous than usual lately.
She still rocks, but she is also beginning to fiddle with
her hands in a nervous manner. I think perhaps the
thought of a job was too much for the girl. She said she
wasn't going to work in the kitchen but she might work in
the cafeteria in the main building. I asked her if she
wanted to work or not and she wasn't quite sure. She is
not used to making decisions on her own. I got the impression, however, that she wasn't very anxious to start
a job.

We played cards again today. Louise played with us
also. The hospital is beginning to depress me more each
week. In the beginning I enjoyed the work and thought I
realized that we might not make much of an impact. Well,
I feel we aren't making too much of an impact on the hospital or the patients. I wonder if my visits are really
helping Ruth. The staff notices her more now but that
seems to be making her nervous. Perhaps after twenty-
three years, change is too great a thing to ask of her.

March 3

Ruth is still nervous, rocking more vigorously and

fiddling around with her fingers. It looks like she isn't going to take any job at all. I wish I knew how her mind works. Is she behaving this way so she won't have to work or is the threat of some responsibility just too much for her?

I was in a bad mood today anyway because of my own problems, and seeing Ruth and the other patients just upset me more. Once I thought I might become a clinical psychologist. I have a great interest in people and like to work among them, not paper and machines. However, my experience at the hospital is slowly changing my mind about a career in psychology. Psychologists don't promise any cure. They talk with patients if they have time and get huge sums for discussing clients' problems. But as far as I can see, problems are seldom solved, relapses occur often, and the work is so frustrating that I don't think I could handle it. Psychology offers few answers and perhaps I need more to calm my own psyche.

March 8

Ruth is still nervous this week. I told the other students with whom I go to the hospital that she's beginning to worry me. It's sad, when she was doing so well, to see her deteriorate. I think she's worse now than she was in September when I first started visiting her. She was pretty good then and I thought she could handle some change. But perhaps after twenty-three years at the hospital she was happily settled and I've just upset her quiet life temporarily.

March 20

Ruth's relapse was completed during this last week. I could see it coming so I can't say it surprised me, although I wish I could have done something to help her. I just didn't know what to do. The staff also noticed her nervousness but I guess they didn't know what to do either, except to wait and see what would happen.

Today when I went to see Ruth she was rocking faster than ever. Her hands were moving too. I walked up to her and put my hand on her shoulder, asking her what was

wrong. She said she couldn't talk to me today. I asked
her how long she had been this nervous; she said awhile
and wouldn't talk any more.

I talked to a nurse, Miss Berg, and she said Ruth
had been this way since Tuesday. Tuesday she was rocking,
etc., and asked to be put in a room alone because she felt
like breaking windows. I don't know if Ruth really would
break the windows or if she knows saying that will cause
the staff to put her in a room alone, away from the
stressful world and the bustling of students and staff.
She was a bit calmer on Wednesday but still more nervous
than usual. Thursday was about like Wednesday and today
she's as bad as she was Tuesday.

Ruth didn't want to talk to me and the cooking class
had to be run so I got some of the patients together.
Meanwhile they gave Ruth a shower and took her away to a
private room. Poor Ruth is a nervous wreck and I can't
take it much longer either. I just visit the hospital
and it drives me up a wall. What about the poor patients
who live there every day? There's got to be a better way.

Next week has got to be better. It's rained every
time I've gone to the hospital for the past three weeks
which is perhaps symbolic of the gloomy days in the hospital. I hope next week is sunny.

March 24

Ruth is on Ward Three now. The ward is stark, depressing, and as Ruth said, "The walls are all around
you." She's calmed down since last week but she didn't
want to go out, to the canteen or even off the ward. I
didn't know what to say to Ruth about last week's behavior. It just happened. Ruth couldn't tell me why; if
she knew maybe she could prevent it.

I hated to have to tell her I wouldn't be coming
next week because of vacation. How could I leave her in
such a mess? The other patients on the ward are really
badly off. It's so depressing. How could anyone possibly feel better on such a terrible ward? We talked
awhile and then I left. I don't feel I'm very useful to
Ruth. I come in and out of her life at weekly intervals
but who knows if it does any good?

March 31 - Vacation

Sent Ruth a card.

April 5

Ruth's back on Two. I feel like we've gone in a complete circle since September, sort of like the business cycle, from prosperity and success to depression and back to the middle again. I wonder how long it will take before Ruth gets another chance to try to make it somewhat on her own.

We went down to the canteen and got a couple of Cokes, then talked in the rotunda. Things are pretty much the same as usual.

Ruth hasn't been coming to cooking class and the only person who seems interested in it is Gail. The other patients who come practically have to be forced to help cook. They just want to eat. I'm beginning to wonder what good, if any, the cooking class is. I don't think any of the patients who attend will be cooking for themselves for a long time, if ever.

April 12

Today, Ruth and I went out for awhile. I told her that soon school would be over and I would be leaving. She didn't appear to be very upset over the fact. I think she knew I'd be leaving for the summer, anyway. I told her I'd write to her if she would write back and let me know how she was doing.

She didn't believe that with all the things I have to do I'd have time to think about her. I assured her that I think of her often and I am concerned about her welfare even though I cannot visit her any longer.

Ruth seemed to take the whole departure scene very well. I wonder how it will be when I really am seeing her for the last time. I have a feeling it will affect me more than her.

April 20

     It was raining today, so Ruth and I stayed in and
played cards. We went down to the canteen for awhile,
too. Nothing really happened. Ruth said she was sick a
couple of days this week--physically sick. She didn't
look so great either. I told her maybe we'd go on a picnic sometime when the weather's good and she said that
would be nice.

April 26

     Ruth said she felt a little sick again this week.
She said she was nervous on Monday but she's better today.
We went down to the canteen and sat awhile. I told Ruth
about a present Ted, a guy she had met twice and whom I
spoke of occasionally, had given me and she asked who Ted
was. She always knew him before; I felt bad that she had
forgotten. I refreshed her memory and she remembers she
had played cards with him and some things about him. We
went back to the ward and played cards; Ruth didn't want
to go out. I was talking about the two remaining weeks
of school and mentioned that I would be happy when my
tests and papers were finished; she added, "And you won't
see me either." I told her that was one of the bad things
about school being over but at least we had had fun together at times. I guess she does feel bad about my
leaving but I suppose it can't be helped.

May 3

     Today we had planned to have a picnic near the hos-
pital for the cooking class and Ruth and Helen but it
rained all day and was cold.

     We picked up some food anyway and had a little party
on the open ward. I will be seeing Ruth only one more
time (I may see her more, but I didn't want to promise
her if I was not sure) and it was kind of a down day. I
felt as though we should have done something special today but we did the same old things--sat, tried to talk,
walked around a little.

A movie was on the T.V. nearby--"The Three Faces of Eve"--and I felt more like watching that than talking to Ruth although I tried not to. I really don't like the idea that I'll be leaving Ruth soon but I'll be very happy to leave Bethlehem. I wish Ruth could be in a halfway house or something similar where I could visit her and we could make some tea or something and sit down at a regular kitchen table to talk. I'd like to see her someplace where there are pleasant surroundings and no locked doors. She really wouldn't be a bad lady to visit, I don't think, if she were back in the "real" world, but I suppose there is no use in hoping for something so doubtful.

May 10

Today was my last visit with Ruth. At last it wasn't raining and we had a chance to walk around and sit outside among the trees and birds. It was a rather nice visit although in the back of our minds we both had the fact that it was our last.

I talked about school ending and Ruth said that when I graduate I'll be really smart. I said I wasn't so sure about that, but I have learned a lot in school. She asked me if I learned anything from Bethlehem.

I told her I learned a lot about institutional life and the way in which it affects the lives of people. We discussed how hard it is to take care of yourself and be independent after years of institutionalization and Ruth added, "Yes, and I've suffered for it." She's right. It's sad to see how her life has been stifled by our system of "treatment" for mentally ill persons. She has suffered. She doesn't enjoy life and will probably never get a chance to. She'll just exist at Bethlehem, probably until she dies.

It wasn't very easy to leave--to say yes, you've suffered, but I'm busy and have to go. Ruth may never get a chance to enjoy life, but at least we can try to prevent other people's lives from being destroyed.

Ruth and I almost cried when we kissed each other and said goodbye. We plan to write and I don't really feel that I won't see her again. As much as I would like to avoid the atmosphere and sickness which Bethlehem generates, I feel that I can't just forget about Ruth. It's often boring and a pain to spend a couple of hours at the hospital but at least, thank goodness, I can walk out and never return if I choose not to.

RUTH STEVENS

FOLLOW-UP INTERVIEW

JP - The reason I asked to talk with you is that
     I'm trying to evaluate the student program
     here at the hospital. Could you tell me
     what you think of it?

     I had a girl who used to come to see me,
     but I don't remember her name.

JP - Was it Debby?

     I think so.

JP - What did you think of the program?

     They have so many people who come here.
     Doctors, students, and others.

JP - What do you remember about the experience
     with Debby?

     I didn't talk much to her or her to me.
     We just sat like some dummies.

JP - How come?

     I don't know. I was sick most of the
     time. She'd have to leave when she
     found out how sick I was.

JP - Do you think she was afraid of you?

     I don't think so.

JP - What do you remember about her?

     I thought she was a nice girl.

JP - Remember what she looked like?

     About my height, long hair, and then
     she had it cut. Looked nice.

JP - Remember anything about what you talked
     about?

     We didn't talk much about anything.

JP - Would you have liked to talk more with her?

     Sometimes I think about her. How she

was getting along. She used to talk about her exams.

JP - Do you know where she is now?

> I think she's back at the university. (Pause) She wrote me a card or a letter. When she left, we kissed each other goodbye and I knew we wouldn't see each other again. I didn't answer the letter.

JP - How come you didn't answer it?

> I was sick <u>most</u> of the time. She wanted to go out in the cold and walk around. We did make some cookies and French toast together. I'd better get back.

JP - Wait a minute.

> I ate some cookies. Some other girls came and ate up the French toast. Brought some cookies back to the ward. Thought the other girls would like them. But they were so good, I ate them all.

JP - How do you think things could have been better between you and Debby?

> I don't know.

JP - Do you think Debby will ever be a patient or get sick?

> I don't know. She's too smart to be in here. She was a smart girl.

JP - Why do you think you're here?

> I don't get along with different people on the outside. My sister, though, comes to see me. We get along pretty well together.

JP - Did you get along with Debby?

> Yes. (Silence)

JP - I get the feeling you don't think you're

too smart.

> This is a hospital for the insane.
> They brought me here and I stay here.
> Was out for a year, though, with my
> sister.

JP - Do you think Debby learned anything from
you?

> No. I don't think so.

JP - Anything about the hospital?

> All kinds of things go on in here.
> They break windows and they holler
> themselves to death.

JP - Why do they do it?

> Because they get upset.

JP - Do you think Debby has a better idea of
that now?

> She gets along with people well. She
> lives with three or four other girls.
> She has to do the cooking besides
> having exams and things like that.

JP - Did Debby get to know you at all?

> No.

JP - Why not?

> I don't know.

JP - Did you trust her?

> Yes.

JP - Was the whole experience worth having?

> Yes.

JP - Why?

> I don't know.

JP - It felt good having someone to visit you.

> Yes.

JP - Did you learn anything from her?

> No.

JP - Do you think she understands people who
     live in mental hospitals better now?

> At the university they learn. She gets
> along all right.

JP - Do you have any children?

> Yes, a daughter.

JP - Did Debby remind you of her?

> Yes.

JP - Would you like to have a daughter like
     Debby?

> Yes.   (Pause)

JP - Why do you rock so much?

> I don't know.

JP - What do you think about when I talk to you
     about Debby? What just made you laugh?

> I don't talk to men very much.

JP - You were having some thoughts about me?

> I guess so.

JP - Want to tell me those thoughts?

> No.

JP - Should we have male students? Would that
     work better?

> No.

JP - You're not so big a conversationalist, are
     you?

> No.

JP - Worried--my writing everything down?

> No.

JP - Sounds like Debby didn't make much of an
     impression on you?

> I don't know. (Pause) Are you through?
> You already wrote three papers.

JP - I just have the feeling more went on and you

aren't telling me.

> She took me downtown in a taxi once.
> With another student too. We had quite
> a time too. Went in every store there
> was. Ate downtown too.

JP - Ever been downtown since?

> I go through the town to my sister's
> house. Sister used to take me down
> every Saturday. Now it's every third
> Saturday.

JP - Ever been into the stores themselves?

> When my sister comes we do.

JP - Do you look forward to these visits?

> Yes.

JP - How old is your daughter?

> Twenty-two.

JP - She ever come to visit you?

> She came once.

JP - You saw Debby more.

> Yes.

JP - How does that make you feel.

> Good. Pretty good.

JP - Wouldn't you like to see your daughter more?

> Yes.

JP - Is it lonely here in the hospital?

> No.

JP - After all Debby's visits, all you have to
say is a couple of words. Yes, no....

> That's right, what you just said.

JP - I guess you don't let people get to know
you?

> No. I stick to my sister.

JP - Would it be disloyal to have other friends?

No.

JP - Are you ashamed of yourself? Is that why
you don't let people know you?

I'm just not a good conversationalist.

JP - Did you get to know Debby?

Yea. Don't make me tell you.

JP - Why?

I figure you're going to send her back
to me.

JP - No. I'm not. You don't want her back?

I don't see why she came in the first
place.

JP - Did you ask her?

I said if she comes back to the university to look me up again.

JP - But she didn't. I don't think she's back.
Sounds like you're disappointed she didn't
look you up. You're mad at her.

(Laughing)

JP - Is that right?

Part of it is. (Looking more friendly)

JP - You thought she'd come back in September.

Yes. (Sadly)

JP - Did you let her know before she left that
you were really looking forward to her
coming back?

Yes.

JP - Why don't you think she came back then?

One of the other students told me about
it. That she is back.

JP - You asked him?

No. He just told me. He's the one who
sent the girls here. I see him practically every day.

JP - Do you have a new student this year?

      No.

JP - Still waiting for Debby?

      Yes.

JP - Is that really so, or are you just telling
me that?

      I practically see her in the hall there,
the way you write about it. (Looking
toward the hall)

JP - You look like you're almost ready to cry?

      No. I'm not.

JP - Just that there's been so few people in
your life, huh?

      Yes. I never did mix much with differ-
ent people.

JP - So. She's one of very few people?

      Yes. I'm going to go back to the bingo
party.

JP - Why do you want to go back to the bingo?
Do you get sad talking about Debby?

      No.

JP - Was she a nice person?

      Yes.

JP - In what way was she nice?

      I don't know. Just nice.

JP - I guess not too many people bother to talk
with you?

      Once in a great while I get to see the
doctor. That's all. You're a doctor
too, aren't you?

JP - Yes. None of the other patients talk much
to you?

      No.

JP - How come?

They have their families. I have mine.

JP - So Debby never knew how much she meant to you?

No. The story of my life.

JP - Want to tell me more about that?

No.

JP - I get the feeling that you suffer a lot.

In here I do.

JP - What makes you suffer the most here?

I feel like hitting the people around me when they upset me and disturb me.

JP - When you get those feelings, does that make you feel bad?

Yes. I break windows.

JP - Did you ever get very mad at Debby?

No.

JP - What makes you mad at the other people?

They don't sit quietly. Always up and around. Quarrel with each other. I can't understand it.

JP - You just sit and rock back and forth.

(Grimacing)

JP - Did that make you mad when I said that?

Yes.

JP - Anyone beside Debby pay attention to you ever?

My mother died seven years ago. Father, he died too. Have a brother and sister.

JP - But here at the hospital? Anyone pay attention to you here?

Not much.

JP - Why?

What is there to talk about? All I get

is something to eat and that's all.

JP - Is it the same for everybody?

I think so.

JP - So the students make a difference?

Yes.

JP - Really? Or are you just trying to make me feel better?

(She starts to cry)

JP - Was that a tear you wiped away?

Yes.

JP - Did you ever let Debby see how sad you are?

Yes. She's seen me.

JP - She saw you cry?

(Shakes head no)

JP - How come you didn't share your sadness with her?

I don't know. Too dumb I guess.

JP - Is it that you only realized how valuable she was after she was gone?

No.

JP - You don't like to let people see how sad you are.

Lots of sad people in this hall.

JP - Were you ever worried about making her sad?

Yes.

JP - Is that why you didn't tell her about your troubles?

I don't know. Lots of times she said she had a paper to do at the university.

JP - I guess you gave her lots of possible excuses so that she could leave if she wanted to?

Yes.

JP - You don't want to impose on anybody?

      No.

JP - Did you have some concern about talking
    with a younger girl?

      I treated her like I do my sister. She
      does the things she thinks I like to
      have done. Makes sure I have enough to
      eat.

JP - So you wanted to be sure Debby wouldn't be
    too sad, or get upset? That's why you
    wouldn't tell her too many strange thoughts
    or sad stories?

      I guess that's it.

JP - But I bet you have a lot of trouble to talk
    about?

      Don't we though.

JP - Could tell a lot of books?

      Yes.

JP - How come you keep all of your experiences
    and thoughts to yourself?

      Some of them I don't think about myself.

JP - It's painful to think about them?

      Yes. Are we through?

JP - What would you want if you had one wish?

      (Long pause) I'd commit suicide.

JP - Why?

      Don't ask me that question.

JP - You know why, but don't want to tell me?

      Yes.

JP - Something you're guilty about. Right?

      Right!

JP - Did you talk with Debby about that?

      No.

JP - With anybody ever?

>No.
>My family is dwindling now. So I think
>I shall die too.

JP - You don't like people to leave you. Huh?

>No.

JP - Sounds like the trouble with Debby is that
she left?

>Yea.

JP - Did anyone offer you another student?

>No.

JP - Did you ask?

>No.

JP - Do you want another student?

>No.

JP - Would you want Debby to come back?

>Yea.

JP - Why don't you let the fellow from the university know you'd like her to come back?

>I don't talk to him.

JP - You want Debby to come back on her own?

>She would never do that. She's got
>other things to do.

JP - No time for you?

>No.

JP - Why not?

>She can come if she wants. Could you
>tell her that I'd like to see her?
>Have her come up here again.

JP - I don't know her.

>But the way you were talking, I thought
>you did.

JP - Why not tell some of the students who visit

now?   Know her last name?

Peters.

JP - Maybe she feels hurt that you didn't answer her letter?

I still have her address.

JP - Ain't got too many other people?

No.

JP - My last question.   You wanted to leave the interview before?

I've been in these buildings for twenty-five years.   I thought I was here long enough.   Out for a year, but I got lonesome at home.   So my sister brought me back.

JP - I mean during this interview.

I didn't want to talk to you.

JP - Why?

I don't know why.

JP - Did it turn out worthwhile?

Yes.

JP - Oh. Let's stop then. Thanks for talking with me.

6

WHY ARE YOU HERE?

Perspectives
on the Bethlehem Experience

In each of five chapters an attempt has been made to reveal the perspective of the institution through material from clinical charts, the perspective of the student from diary entries, and the patient's perspective as it emerges in an interview conducted almost a year after the relationship had formally ended. If the attempt was successful the reader has shared in the institution's view of the patient, the student's view of self, patient, and institution, and the patient's view of self, student, and institution.

What general conclusions about student-patient relationships may be drawn from the specific instances presented in these chapters? What conclusions may be reached, given the selective and subjective nature of the data? The hospital charts are representative of the records kept by state mental hospitals, and are perhaps above average in attempts at detail and regularity of description. Did the students tell it like it was? Their diaries were kept regularly, are reasonably candid and open, and correspond to the issues and problems they brought to the weekly support group. At times, one wishes that a student had continued a self-analysis or described in more detail something she found unpleasant. The reader may recognize much that the student and patient appeared unready to see. But we do not claim that the diaries are comprehensive in their insight or that

they are completely candid, without defenses on the students' part; instead they are accepted as true and honest
presentations of the students' experience. Correspond-
ingly, in the interviews the patients for the most part
describe the students and the hospital experience with
emotion and clarity.

We believe it is legitimate to attempt to understand
five atypical interpersonal relationships by analyzing
the intersubjectivity of diary and interview. In doing
so, we have considered also the experience of other students in the course as conveyed in diaries and support
group discussions. What did students and patients bring
to the relationships, what meanings did the relationships
have for them, and what did the participants gain? In
attempting to answer these questions one is compelled to
consider contrasting perspectives on the mental hospital
experience, and to think about the meaning of mental illness, the ways in which it is defined, and the responses
it creates.

In order to better define these relationships we
have divided the student-patient work year into three
parts--an orientation period, a working period, and a
termination period. For our analysis, stages are determined not by a fixed number of visits, but by sequences
of demands and crises that emerge in the student-patient
interactions.

ORIENTATION PERIOD

The students enter the institution with the super-
ficially defined role of counselor-companion, and with
only brief course preparation to help reduce fearful pre-
conceptions of mental illness and mentally ill patients.
Even so, students receive more orientation than do the
patients, and have a longer time to anticipate the relationship. Students sign up for the course three months
before it begins; at that time they participate in an
orientation meeting at the university, then share at
least one class meeting and a support group before a further orientation at the hospital. Then they meet the
patients. The patients, on the other hand, are chosen by
hospital directors in the days and weeks before the
course begins, and a few appear surprised to find that
they have a student visitor.

PROBLEMS AT ENTRY   The first problems the students experience are fear, and apprehensions about accepting and
being accepted. In some student diaries, there is a
sense that entering the institution carries an almost
ritual status, that it is an initiation into a feared
world, and perhaps into a new level of personal maturity
as well. Students may experience fear of doing harm to
an emotionally vulnerable patient, as well as fear of
being harmed; students may find it difficult to justify
their intervention in the life of a chronic patient,
given their lack of clinical experience. This course and
others of its kind are innovative in asserting that institutionalized mental patients are still members of the
community and that contact with them is not the restricted
province of trained professionals. The mental patient's
extreme defeat and stigmatization, the student's compen-
sations for these and awe of mental illness, professional
labeling practices and overarching protectiveness--all of
these circumstances result in the patient and student
coming face to face afraid to ask each other the immediate and obvious question, "Why are you here?"

Students begin a lengthy struggle to define their
role in the new setting. Initially, their relationships
with the patients are bound by no explicit contract beyond a commitment to see patients weekly for nine months
and the understanding that the patients can refuse to see
them. In their need for a human equation by which to
pursue the relationships, the students, in an untutored
way, value and seek to convey empathy, acceptance, and
openness; they seem to assume that the patient's predica-
ment may be caused at least in part by a lack of these
qualities in past relationships. Their lack of clinical
training or experience leads them to adopt the role of
friend or the vague but given role of counselor-companion,
rather than one of therapist, or what they see as a therapist's role.

The responsibility assumed by the students to show
empathy and to be accepting and open, and their commitment to stay with the relationships for the duration of
the academic year, distinguish them from typical companions or friends, however. The students' intense apprehension as meetings with their patients approach, and its
resemblance to the anxiety of a first date, suggests that
the relationship has special importance in a variety of

ways. At first some see the experience as a test for
career aptitude. The intense need to do well may reveal
itself as a cure fantasy, the other side of which is fear
of doing harm. Further, the student may feel the forthcoming relationship with a patient will be a test of self-
worth and identity, as if this commitment to another may
provide a true measure of how closely the student fulfills
his or her self-ideals; in fact this relationship will
test the ability to act responsibly toward another person, sometimes at the expense of self-idealizations, such
as always liking others in all their perceived inadequa-
cies. Students who persist in trying to relate to a patient who pleads helplessness and flees into symptoms
inevitably learn that they themselves can be "mean," that
their own needs often take precedence and that this is
better acknowledged; acknowledged feelings allow choice
in actions. The necessity to honestly recognize a range
of intense feelings may evoke in the student great anxiety, as well as anger that the relationship requires so
much essential work (in the diarists' terms, the friendship is so one-way). Ellen and Jane particularly had to
cope with their anger at patient self-centeredness or
lack of progress, and eventually they recognized limitations in their own powers of acceptance. Amy, in contrast, more easily realized that there were many of Ann's
attributes that she found unpleasant and could not accept.

Through determination to recognize their own feelings
and evaluate their own responses in relationship to patients, students may encourage patients to increase their
awareness and self-acceptance. The course structure,
with diary and support group, demands openness to experiential learning--a willingness to share one's experience,
examine one's behavior, and self-correct. The students
learn by trial and error that they can often best fulfill
a helping function by disregarding assumptions they may
have about the kinds of help patients want and need, and
by distinguishing the requirements of a helping companionship from those of friendship. These helping relationships are work. They demand self-evaluation at all
stages of the relationship. While the relationships
themselves are the object of the students' visits to the
institution, they are as goal-directed as each student's
definition of them. More will be said later about the
helper-friend definition; for now it is sufficient to

point out that students and patients evolve relationships within the role and physical restrictions imposed by student-patient status differences. Friendships have probably evolved and survived in the face of greater obstacles, but one would expect this rarely, in contrast to the students' expectations. One could safely predict some hard coming to terms with reality over the course of the year. The extent to which student progress is made at the patient's expense is an important question.

To the patient it may initially come as a surprise that he or she has a visitor. Not knowing why the institution has singled him or her out for such attention, it is not clear whether the patient perceives this latest development as a threat or a blessing, and it is unknown whether he or she feels, in relation to the institution, that a choice is possible in the matter. A few patients do refuse at the start to enter relationships with students. But within relationships both student and patient have innumerable escapes and protections. The diaries and interviews bear this out. At no time does the experience appear to degenerate into an inescapable ordeal for either patient or student; at worst the patient's conversation may slip into a bizarre, crazy, or nonsensical style, or the student may feel frustrated and ineffective, may find conversation difficult, and a visit boring or depressing. A patient's illogical speech, commonly interpreted as flight from an intolerable situation, just as often seems to be an oblique test of a student's capacity to acknowledge and cope with feelings. Most students must do considerable emotional work before they can bear to face the harsh realities of institutionalized patients' lives; witness the contrast between students' adamant refusals to give up hope in many instances and the patients' tone of inevitability in the interview material.

PROBLEMS OF RELATING   Upon first meeting, and sometimes for as long as they know each other, student and patient may feel they have little to talk about. They may have no immediate common ground on which to build a relationship. Their pairing is random, except for sex matching. The patient's status as mental patient, the most fundamental reason for the relationship and its setting, may itself be perceived by one or both parties as highly

sensitive and threatening. In periods of economic depression and joblessness people are afraid to start
friendly conversation by asking, "What do you do?" Similarly, in the hospital an unspeakable present may severely inhibit talk of past and future as well. The patient's
past is often one of interpersonal brutality and social
failure, as the hospital records indicate; recognition of
student youth and inexperience, and fear of the student's
unpredictable reactions to feelings and experiences which
are still a source of anxiety and guilt to the patient,
may inhibit a patient's conversation. A student made
anxious by a patient's past and present may be reluctant
to probe, attributing this to fear of touching patient
sensitivities.

The students seldom adequately explain to the patients their intentions in visiting, perhaps because of
their own uncertainty about what is to come. To say to
the patient that one is there to help may promise more
than the student is sure he or she can deliver and imply
a status difference the student is unwilling to acknowledge. To make known the limitations of one's commitment,
as the student must, even if she or he leaves open the
possibility of a continuing relationship, is antithetic
to the spontaneity many of the students feel a need for.
It is no wonder that conversation is very constrained,
that it often seems there is little to talk about. Students frequently attribute the conversational void to the
emptiness of the patient's existence, but silence comes
as much from the students' intimidation by an institution
standing on a hill in formidable authority and isolation,
and the personification, however mild, of some of the
students' most fearful fantasies. In everyday terms, interaction with the patient, with its absence of social
conventions, may present to the student reflections of
personal dishonesty, status needs, intolerance of differences, and lack of commitment.

ACCEPTANCE   At entry each student's apprehension seems
focused on her need to be accepted by the patient. This
need takes on all the intensity and emotional turmoil of
previous situations characterized by the insecurity and
uncertainty of possibly meeting with rejection from a
significant person, only now the consequences of rejection are magnified by the student's anxiety to do well

and the necessity of relying on the self in the absence
of a defined role. If the student finds herself accepted,
as most are, her self-confidence may be enhanced and she
may begin to define realistic goals for the relationship.

In contrast, patients appear to view the relationship as less of a problem at the outset, with few excep-
tions. Alicia seems driven to impress and control; Ann
seems eager to talk about herself. Most of the patients
simply let the students initiate the relationships, perhaps assuming that the students are there to learn about
mental patients; few seem overtly worried about the first
impression they make, or seem to see the students as particularly threatening. A few take emotional risks, others make no apparent effort to contribute to the relationship's development or direction.

The students, concerned about being accepted, strive
to be accepting themselves. Initially they often over-
look or fail to see disordered behavior, ostensibly wish-
ing to be completely tolerant and not to stereotype others; confronted by undeniably illogical speech, they are
uncertain how to respond, short of rejecting the other's
experience. Jane, for example, abruptly became aware of
her attempts to normalize strange behavior in her desire
to accept mental patients. Initially she failed to acknowledge the illogical content of a patient's conversation; one moment she was nodding in agreement, the next
she did a doubletake when the patient (Alicia) pointed to
the window and said, "Here comes Lassie now!"

As students' initial anxiety diminishes they gradually cease to deny abnormal behavior. Students work to
overcome fears of being harmed and doing harm, grow to
accept persons very different from themselves, and learn
unambiguous ways of communicating acceptance. Student
anxiety later in the experience seems more closely related to questions of identification, trust, responsibility, and developing self-knowledge.

WORKING PERIOD

Students may perceive abnormal behavior not as growing from a pathological process in the individual but as
a role normal to the institutional setting. If the students do not totally reject the illness model of psycho-

pathology, they in any case set it aside, perhaps as irrelevant to their efforts.

The ordinariness of most of a patient's behavior
often leads a student to wonder why a patient is not outside the hospital working or why the student (or a friend
or relative) is not considered abnormal and hospitalized.
The student's questioning of a patient's institutional
status and diagnostic label often takes the form, "Why
him (or her) and not me?" or simply, "Why not me?" Later
on when the student recognizes instances of deviant behavior that he or she previously had not acknowledged,
the questioning of a patient's status may change. Recognized similarities between the patient and the student
which originally were indications that "he is as normal
as I" may now lead to the other possibility that "I am as
abnormal as he." These questions can be a source of anxiety, and the student's struggle to resolve them may provide significant movement toward self-definition. Amy's
diary provides examples as she tried to understand how
she and Ann were alike and different. Another student,
not represented in the present collection, wrote in his
course diary, "...identifying with the person, it got to
the point where I had to ask myself where I was different
from him. In short, I was defining myself more and
more..." (Golann, Baker & Frydman, 1973). Even when the
student's identification with a patient is not close,
questions of similarities and differences may be puzzling.

Patients too make many comparisons, remembering what
they were like or how they felt when they were young.
They evaluate social change from what little they see of
the students' lives. Perhaps in this way they see the
course of their own lives in a new light. Just as students cannot help perceiving themselves through the patients' eyes, patients cannot always help perceiving
themselves somewhat through the students' eyes. In
learning more about each other, student and patient encounter fear about themselves, and may be led to more
realistic self-evaluations. At this time the patient may
begin to care more than before what the student thinks of
him or her as a person.

ACKNOWLEDGING AND DEALING WITH FEELINGS   In the working
period of the relationship students often experience
feelings of anger, frustration, and depression. Hopeful-

ness can turn into hopelessness when students are forced
to cope with extremely slow progress, the setbacks and
regressions of their patients, and the chronic nature of
patient problems. Karen's moods fluctuated radically in
response to Alicia's progress and setbacks; because she
did not want to give up hope that she could help Alicia
get out of the hospital, she ended the year feeling
crushed, overwhelmed, and angry, though perhaps more
seasoned in her battle of hope versus despair. Debby's
diary also shows her becoming progressively more discouraged, even though from the relationship's start she had
questions about how she could help. Fantasies of cure
are effectively exploded by the slow development of relationships. Students may attribute lack of change in a
patient's behavior, and difficulties in involving a patient in new activities or spontaneous and meaningful
conversations, to the patient's uncompromising attitude.
Others may begin to suspect that their own needs, limitations, fears, and impatience may be real barriers to the
relationship's growth.

When a student's personal relationships outside the
hospital are going badly, and he finds himself looking
toward his institutionalized companion for support, his
disappointment and depression may deepen. As far as the
patients are concerned, they are the reasons for and the
continuing foci of these relationships. No one likes to
be left behind or left out, and the patients seemingly
wish to forget that the students have outside lives. But
students become angry at having their own needs ignored
and rejected. Ellen's and Karen's diaries provide ample
illustrations of this. The students also complain that
it is draining when they must always sustain the interest
and enthusiasm in the relationships, when they are always
the initiators. In contrast to the student position, the
patients seem to have a much clearer idea of what their
own responsibilities are and are not in these relationships. They are the patients.

At times, students and patients apparently expect
one another to be able to read minds, to respond sympathetically to unspoken needs. As relationships increase
in emotional meaning and intensity, the burden of the unspoken grows particularly heavy. While the student sulks
because the patient never shows any interest in her life,
and perhaps meets the obligations of her commitment re-

luctantly or resentfully, the patient may resent the student's failures to understand her problems and feelings, while being jealous of a student's attentions to other patients, irritated at a student's bids for control and prods for change, and fearful of rejection by the student now that an attachment has formed. Sometimes these binding relationships resemble friendships, but often they remind one of marriage.

THE INSTITUTION AS THIRD PARTY   When students first enter the institution they seem prepared to meet the frightening psychotics of popular fantasy; instead, touched by the patients' dependence and loneliness, most respond sympathetically; finally most of the students come to see the patients as persons with vastly underrated potentials. The stubborn endurance and great depth of the patients' helplessness and dependence, their apparent egocentricity (distinguished from that of the students by the patients' status as patients, and their apparent indifference to the conventions of social interaction), and of course their generally schizophrenic symptomatology, remain the greatest mystery to the students who have recognized the ordinariness of their needs.

Most students now seek to define how the institution is implicated in patients' problems, especially as they begin to suspect that the chronic and forgotten patients are quite incapable of leaving. At one time or another most students seem to view withdrawn patients as people who have been hurt repeatedly in profound ways, then driven to schizophrenic oblivion by years of institutional maintenance. As an explanation for the patient's indisposition to change, however, the concept of institutional bondage is incomplete. Patients unable or unwilling to cope with noninstitutional life share at least some responsibility for remaining in an institution. Family relationships may have contributed to a patient's deviant status and institutionalization, and with his contribution may still maintain him there. These factors are hidden from the student's view, however, whereas the institution is omnipresent. For the patient to reveal outside dynamics to the student may threaten the patient with loss of a status quo. However, the patient may trust the student to intervene in or do

battle with the immediate setting, where little is likely
to change.

The institution first becomes a source of frustration to the students because of its regimentation, con-
tradictory goals, and the seeming insensitivity of staff
toward patients. Although quite neutral to the institution and its rules at the beginning of the program, the
students later describe the institution as a stigmatizing
setting characterized by no privacy, no treatment, rigid
rules, insensitivity to patient needs and feelings, con-
descension, low expectations, and depressing impersonality. As a treatment setting they see it reinforcing only
dependency, incompetence, and schizophrenic behavior.
Ellen's diary is vivid on this point and she wonders how
long it takes before impersonal superficiality affects
one's self-concept. Debby and Ruth quietly discuss how
the hospital environment has been bad for Ruth. Ann,
after thirty-two years in the hospital, tells us, "You
get used to everything."

The student experiencing difficulty in developing
and maintaining a relationship with a patient can and
does blame this in part on the debilitating, custodial
institutional climate. Many students, after only brief
contact with it, describe the institution as intensely
depressing and energy-depleting. Even when overt conflict is not apparent, the institution remains a silent
third party to all transactions between student and patient. The student determined to develop a relationship
approximating the mutuality of friendship often finds
himself or herself competing with the institution which
has promised the patient food, asylum, bed, and safety at
the expense of independence and self-responsibility. It
is true that retrieving a patient from years of such institutionalization is like trying to rescue Jonah from
the whale after he has been partially digested, and it is
no wonder that the institution becomes the target of student puzzlement and anger.

When students' opinions and feelings collide directly with institutional policy and staff decisions concerning their patients, students moderate their expressions
of frustration and anger in order to negotiate with the
staff on the patients' behalf; sometimes in the process
they attempt to provide patients with models of diplomacy

under stress. Within the student-patient-institution
triangle, however, highly complicated tensions sometimes
develop, calling into question a student's trustworthiness and allegiance. Student and staff may think a patient should leave the institution when the patient
doesn't want to, leading the patient to question whose
side the student is on. Or a patient moved back a ward
may blame the staff and demand the student's complete
concurrence; the staff presumes that the student understands the therapeutic necessity for back ward placement;
the student may be angry at both patient and staff: at
the patient for acting in a manner that led to the setback, at the staff for punishing the patient. Should the
student choose to mediate, as many do to secure patient
gains, she may find herself on behalf of the staff and
despite her own objections, conveying to the patient
necessity for a compromise.

RELATIONSHIP DEFINITION   Partly in response to the loneliness of the patients' lives and the artificiality of
the institutional setting, and partly in reaction to
their own growing need for closeness and acceptance, many
students try to provide patients with relationships approximating friendships, relationships demanding at least
a limited and natural give-and-take. When at a loss for
what to do or say, they seem to ask themselves not, "What
is therapeutically appropriate," but rather, "How would a
friend respond?" When they hear themselves referring to
"my patient" many students correct themselves and say "my
friend." They are bothered not by the possessiveness of
the phrase, but by the status differences and special responsibilities implied in referring to their institutionalized companions as their patients.

Defining their relationships with patients as friendships, however, creates confusions and contradictions the
students must eventually resolve. Does being a friend
mean abandoning rehabilitative aspirations not directly
voiced by the patient? If student companions are friends
do they have the right to urge patient friends to change
themselves or their way of life? Fear of causing patients
emotional pain after twenty or thirty years of institutional isolation is tempered by the conviction that some
pain is a consequence of living and that no one has the
right to protect another from this. On the other hand,

it is likely that the students themselves have experienced resentments when expected to conform to others' expectations. They seem to wonder if remaining institutionalized isn't, after all, just a different way of life. They express anger at society for not accepting a patient's differences; witness especially Karen toward the end of her diary. Perhaps the students, critical of much in adult cultural patterns of interpersonal relationships and values, see the student-patient relationship as a testing ground on which they have the chance to see what might happen if they, rather than their parents' generation, were the culture bearers.

In time, often after considerable vascillation between extremes, the students usually do come to define their roles as involving some measure of responsibility for helping patients move toward more independent, varied, and, in the students' scheme of things, interesting and acceptable life patterns. To extend unasked-for friendship to chronically rejected persons, particularly time-limited friendship, is a difficult task. Students attempt to cope through insight, persistence, and increasing self-acceptance and acceptance of others.

Earlier we mentioned the anger and frustration students may experience when a patient fails to reciprocate friendship adequately or fails to share a student's relationship definitions. Students setting friendship goals are forced sooner or later to see their own needs, and they usually revise their definitions accordingly. Similarly, students are forced to consider responsibly their own needs and limitations as they open themselves to and become involved in issues bearing heavily on the patient's future and the future of the relationship. Each of the diarists thought about how close she and the patient could or should try to become. A student may feel, correctly or not, that her more substantial commitment or contribution can prove vitally important to a patient, but find herself unwilling to take on additional responsibility. By defining the limitations of her commitment she can begin to recognize the patient's existing life choices as they really are, and possibly help the patient to make the best of them.

An overcommitted or overinvolved helper who is unwilling to recognize his own limitations and needs is

likely to become angry, disillusioned, and unrealistical-
ly demanding of a patient. Put somewhat differently, a
patient wanting more than a student can give, or a student wanting to help more than he is able, may contribute
to a situation in which either makes escalating demands
that drive the other away. The students are correct when
they recognize early in the program that growth and insight occur only in a setting of acceptance and trust,
never as a result of impatience or demands. Unfortunately this seems to be a lesson that people have to relearn
many times.

TERMINATION PERIOD

The end of the academic year brings the need for realistic assessment of progress, which is usually small,
and acknowledgment of both the limitedness and importance
of the relationship. With the passage of time and lower-
ing of barriers the relationship between student and patient may have deepened in significance for both. Many
times the relationship is between the young student and
an older person--often the patient has been hospitalized
more years than the student has been alive--and student
and patient may sometimes relate as son or daughter with
parent. The two share a depth of feeling that may surprise them, even though at some point the relationship
may have stopped growing. What student and patient have
experienced is not readily characterized as friendship or
therapy.

As a result of the program, the student is open potentially to diverse experiential learning processes,
possibly producing accelerated personality change and
cognitive growth. Being accepted by a significant other
person may lead to feelings of increased self-worth.
Testing one's own capacity for acceptance under very demanding circumstances may lead to realistic revision of
one's ideals and self. Self-assurance may be gained when
one sees that untutored efforts are not harmful to vulnerable people and can be helpful at times. Serving effectively as a model to other persons, thereby helping
them to deal with their problems, may lead to new and
more effective ways of dealing with one's own problems.
Working to understand a patient, oneself, and the differences between the two may lead to heightened self-aware-

ness, sensitivity, and self-analytical ability. By recognizing unrealistic goals and setting obtainable ones, the student can formulate a more accurate definition of his or her own direction and objectives in life. Resolving intertwined relationships of self, patient, and institution may lead to an understanding of one's actions in the context of their social consequences and to a more effective channeling of strong feelings. Hopefully, from the experience of acting responsibly toward one person, the student will become more adept at defining his or her own limitations and responsibilities in general. Effectively testing new behaviors may lead to increased learning flexibility, attention to feedback, and self-correction.

In addition, through their hospital experience, coordinated course work, and related readings, students more clearly understand the differing perspectives on concepts of normality and abnormality; they learn about the structure and dynamics of a state mental hospital, develop a practical interest in the sociology of deviance and community alternatives to mental institutionalization, and better define their own career goals.

Perhaps less learning and change occurs for the patient, although a few did seem more independent and less in need of student support toward year's end. The chronicity of patient problems is in marked contrast to the students' young, emergent status, and the institutional setting is inconducive to change, unlike the university. There is also a large difference between seeing and being seen, between leaving and being left. The relationship, however, does open a number of areas for patient change, many paralleling those already ennumerated in the previous paragraphs examining student growth. Increased self-worth may result from being accepted by a significant other person; possibly the patient's self-assurance grows when he sees that he is not harming a young and inexperienced student. The patient has the opportunity to compare himself to the student, perhaps better understanding himself and his circumstances in the process. In addition, a patient's contact with a student is a minimal but enlightening contact with the society outside, and potentially an access route to buried memories and forgotten potentials. Perhaps most important, the long-institutionalized person may learn from contact with a student

that he can gain comfort and strengthened human identity
by allowing another to enter his loneliness. Hopefully,
becoming involved in a relationship after years of isolation will be an impetus to further efforts at relating.

In their year together students and patients deal at
various levels with the same themes: fearing rejection,
being lonely, hiding true feelings to "protect the other,"
expecting needs to be satisfied when there is no reason
to believe they will be, coping with mixed feelings about
one another, and struggling with issues of intimacy, independence, and responsibility. It is noteworthy that
the students themselves are members of an institution,
"inmates" of a large state university. While the university has learning and growth as its goals, and it attempts to prepare students for adult roles in the outside
world, the quality of emotional learning it offers and
the extent of its contact with the rest of the community
are often called into question by students and others.
Whatever the merits or failures of the state university
and the students who call upon its resources, students,
pursuing education because of social pressure while unsure of their plans after graduation, may feel that the
university is fostering dependency and ask themselves,
"Why am I here?"

Not surprisingly, both students and patients seem to
have given thought to their similarities and differences,
looking for some explanation of the very divergent life
circumstances which, curiously, brought them together.
From the students' perspective the patients may lack not
only ambition, but also opportunity in life. And as two
of the patients describe them, their students have not
only the opportunities that love, money, education,
friends, and freedom bring, but they have good potentials
because they study to be somebody, extend trust, and have
confidence and a "way with themselves and others." These
perceptions of each other offered by students and patients are more a footnote to their year's experience together than an analysis of why some stay locked away
while others are free. The significance is, at relationship's end, that students and patients do not dehumanize
what they seek to explain.

DISCUSSION QUESTIONS

AMY AND ANN

Amy became upset when Ann showed her the newspaper article about motorcycle accidents. Amy thought it odd that Ann showed her this particular article. What do you think Amy was thinking?

Why do you think Amy didn't want Ann to see her get upset about the newspaper article?

When Ann became openly angry at her, Amy wrote, "It was really great! Ann was taking out some of her hostility on me." How do you think Ann perceived Amy's attempts to arbitrate Ann's relationship with the hospital?

Amy described herself as "just a plain old scared college student...prepared for any shock that might be coming." Do you think Ann perceived her in this way?

Do you think Ann meant it when she told Amy to go away? Should Amy have complied?

Amy placed more emphasis on the differences between Ann and herself than she did on the similarities. Why would she take this approach, and did her emphasis influence the quality of the relationship?

Amy described Ann as "lazy, bossy and catty...and generally quite a bore to be with." What do you think of this description?

Can Amy's need to "act like a nice little girl" around Ann be attributed to Ann's limitations?

Do you think Amy assumed goals for Ann without consulting or listening to her sufficiently? In general, why is it important that students recognize their own needs in a relationship with a patient?

Amy bargained for privileges for Ann, and pushed against the institutional machinery to clear the way for Ann's release. Do you think that Ann could have left the institution without Amy's help if she wished? Why might someone choose to remain in a mental hospital rather than leave?

How did the hospital authorities react to Ann's aggression? Note the chain of feelings after Ann was put on a back ward for arguing. From this chapter, what can be learned about the power of the institution and its staff over the patient? About the "counterpower" of the patient? Where did Amy come into this balance of power? How do you change the interrelationship between institution and patient when neither is ready to change?

Do you think that the successes and failures of Amy and Ann's relationship were their shared responsibility? How did the institution share in this interaction?

ELLEN AND MARY

Mary asked JP, "Am I odd?" Do you think her problems were odd, or were the ways she defined and tried to cope with them odd? Consider, for example, how Ellen and Mary each coped with fears of having the power to hurt the other. In what ways did Mary's and Ellen's styles of coping differ?

What are the things Mary did or said that would be described as manifestations of depression? Throughout her diary, Ellen described experiences that made her feel depressed--what are the differences between Mary's and Ellen's feelings of depression? Did they cope with or use these feelings differently?

What were some of the barriers to Ellen and Mary's becoming close? It helps to imagine yourself in Ellen's and Mary's positions. Did the two of them together regulate the closeness of their relationship? In what ways

did both do this? What were some of the external circumstances impinging on their relationship?

When Mary complimented Ellen extravagantly, why might
this have made Ellen uncomfortable (aside from Ellen's
fear that she might "goof")?

Do you feel that the parties in this relationship profited
unequally? To what would you attribute such an imbalance?

How did Ellen discover for herself the "vicious circle" of
some interpersonal relationships--where fear of something
leads people to act in a way that brings on the very thing
they fear, so their fear grows, and the cycle continues?

After reading Ellen's and Amy's diaries, can you distinguish some of the ways a helping relationship between
student and patient differs from a friendship? Friendships often take the form of reciprocal helping; what is
meant by reciprocity, or dialogue, in friendship?

Ellen ended her diary feeling that Mary had truly trusted
her for the first time. Also she wrote that it was the
first time she had tried to see things Mary's way instead
of trying to make Mary see her way. Are the two events
related?

After telling JP that she hears voices, Mary added, "There
is something mechanically wrong with my head. It's not my
fault." Why might she have said this? Who might be likely to agree or disagree with her?

CAROL AND JANE

In her first diary entry Carol reported that she found
herself normalizing bizarre behavior--she recognized a
discrepancy between the scene she was observing and her
initial perception of it. What do you think is the source
of such distortion? Does it serve a need?

All in all, Carol seemed relieved to find that the hospital was not as fearful a place as she had imagined. How
do you envision a mental hospital?

How does Jane seem to feel about not being very smart?
How do you feel about the interviewer asking her that?
If you were JP, what questions would you have asked Jane
and why?

In her interview with JP, Jane talked about her voices

and what they said to her. One interpretation of hearing
"voices" is that it places the source of unacceptable
feelings outside oneself. What different explanation
might you give for Jane's voices?

When Carol left for the last time, Jane seemed not to
care much. How would you feel if the person you worked
with all year acted as if she didn't care?

KAREN AND ALICIA

Do you get a different picture of Alicia's moods and behavior from reading the chart than you do from the interview?

Karen tried to share Alicia's moods. Are there other
ways she effectively could have helped Alicia?

Alicia said in her interview, "I know she has empathy for
me, but I don't want followers." What did she mean? Do
you think that because of their differences either Karen
or Alicia felt abandoned? Did one experience abandonment
more strongly that the other? Is this a problem in a
helping relationship? In a friendship?

Do you think Alicia, any more than Mary, could be willed,
or could will herself, to behave differently?

Would our perspective on this case be enhanced if we knew
more about Alicia's family?

Do you think that Alicia's hospitalization reflects society's unwillingness to accept divergent values? Does ad-
vocating innovations in the definition, care, and treatment of mental patients' problems necessarily imply a
denial of the reality and severity of their problems?

DEBBY AND RUTH

How would you describe the way Debby defined her relationship with Ruth? Did she care about Ruth more or less than
the other students cared about those whom they visited?

Do you feel that Debby's efforts as an advocate for Ruth
within the institution were sensitive to Ruth's needs?
Such sensitivity is best measured not so much by an absence of errors, as by a student's ability to recover and
learn from errors. How does this relate to setting
shorter-term goals for patient gains?

Note how Debby handled the termination of her relationship with Ruth, and compare this with the methods used by
other students. Do you think it is important that such
relationships be clearly defined and terminated? If you
were to write a student-patient work contract, how would
it read?

Do your feelings differ as you read each section in this
chapter--Ruth's hospital chart, Debby's diary, and the
interview with Ruth?

REFERENCES

Bateson, G., Jackson, D.D., Haley, J., and Weakland, J.H.
   Toward a theory of schizophrenia. *Behavioral Science*,
   1956, 1, 251-264.
Brigham, A. Moral treatment in American psychiatry.
   American Journal of Insanity, 1847, 1-15.
Foucault, M. *Madness and civilization*. New York:
   Pantheon, 1965. (Paperback edition, Random House,
   Vintage, 1973.)
Goffman, E. *Asylums: Essays on the social situation of
   mental patients and other inmates*. Garden City,
   N.Y.: Doubleday, 1961.
Golann, S.E., and Eisdorfer, C. Mental health and the
   community: The development of issues. In S.E.
   Golann and C. Eisdorfer (eds.), *Handbook of commun-
   ity mental health*. New York: Appleton-Century-
   Crofts, 1972.
Golann, S.E., Baker, J., and Frydman, A.A. Demands and
   coping in the undergraduate therapeutic-companion
   experience. *American Journal of Community Psychology*, 1973, 1, 228-237.
Goodman, G. *Companionship therapy: Studies in structured
   intimacy*. San Francisco: Jossey-Bass, 1972.
Grob, G.N. The state mental hospital in mid-nineteenth
   century America: A social analysis. *American Psychologist*, 1966, 21, 510-523.
Haley, J. An interactional description of schizophrenia.
   Psychiatry, 1959, 22, 321-332.

Holzberg, J.D., Knapp, R.H., and Turner, J.L. Companionship with the mentally ill: Effect on the personalities of college student volunteers. *Psychiatry*, 1966, <u>29</u>, 395-405.

Joint Commission on Mental Illness and Health. *Action for mental health*. New York: Basic Books, 1961.

Laing, R.D. *The politics of experience*. Middlesex, England: Penguin Books, 1967.

Rappaport, J., Chinsky, J., and Cowen, E. *Innovations in helping chronic patients: College students in a mental institution*. New York: Academic Press, 1971.

Rosen, G. *Madness in society*. New York: Harper and Row, 1968.

Umbarger, C.C., Dalsimer, J.S., Morrison, A.P., and Breggin, P.R. *College students in a mental hospital*. New York: Grune & Stratton, 1962.

Watzlawick, P., Beavin, J.H., and Jackson, D.D. *Pragmatics of human communication: A study of interactional patterns, pathologies, and paradoxes*. New York: Norton, 1967.

Zilboorg, G., and Henry, G.W. *A history of medical psychology*. New York: Norton, 1941.

GLOSSARY

ACUTE SCHIZOPHRENIC EPISODE   Another term for schizophrenic reaction. The emphasis is on elaborate, bizarre
ideas and behavior.

AFFECTIVITY   Susceptibility to emotional stimuli. Also
used as a synonym for mood or state of feeling.

ANXIETY REACTION   A formal term to indicate the presence
of an anxiety neurosis. The clinical characteristics include general irritability, anxious expectation, pangs of
conscience, and unreasonable fears.

ARTANE   A medicine utilized to reduce side effects of
the potent tranquilizers and antipsychotic drugs.

BENADRYL   An antihistamine medication.

CATATONIA   Characterized by stupor, associated with
either marked rigidity or flexibility of the musculature.
Strange body postures are assumed and maintained without
noticeable movement, or there may be overactivity and extreme excitement. Most often interpreted as a symptom of
schizophrenia.

CONVERSION REACTION   A form of neurosis typified by very
apparent physical symptoms, such as blindness or paralysis, without an actual physical cause.

DEFENSES   Mental mechanisms which serve to protect unacceptable, unconscious thoughts and impulses from reaching
conscious awareness.

225

DELUSIONS   Unique false beliefs maintained despite obvious proof to the contrary.

DENUDATIVE   From denude--to make naked or bare.

DEPRESSIVE REACTION   A neurosis characterized by conscious suffering and guilt.

DISSOCIATIVE REACTION   A type of neurosis often typified by double or multiple personalities. One subpersonality is completely ignorant of the others. Dream states and prolonged sleepwalking trances are also examples of dissociative reactions.

ECT   Electric convulsive treatment. See ELECTRIC SHOCK TREATMENT.

EDEMATOUS AND CYANOTIC   Swelling and a bluish tinge of color.

EDENTULOUS   Without teeth.

ELECTRIC SHOCK TREATMENT (Also, Electric Convulsive Treatment or ECT)   The administration of a measured electric current through two electrodes placed on the skin of the head. It is used in certain depressions and other disorders.

EMOTIONAL LABILITY   Unstable state of mood or feeling. One mood changing rapidly to another. Often a symptom of mania or schizophrenia.

EQUANIL   A mild tranquilizer.

ETIOLOGICAL   Causative. Relating to cause or explanation of disease or problem.

FLIGHT OF IDEAS   A near-continuous flow of speech which is not disjointed or bizarre but which jumps rapidly from one topic to another. Such speech is characteristic of manic states.

HALFWAY HOUSE   A specialized residence for mental patients who are not sick enough to require full hospitalization, but not well enough to function completely within the community without some degree of supervision, protection, and support.

HALLUCINATIONS   Imaginary sensations usually in the form of voices or visions.

HYDRAGARGYRUM PILLS   A hydragogue medicine is usually a

cathartic or diuretic.

HYDROTHERAPY   The treatment of disease by water, administered internally or externally. Such measures are no longer an accepted method of psychiatric treatment.

HYPOCHONDRIA   Overconcern and attention to the details of body functioning and/or exaggeration of any symptom, no matter how insignificant.

HYPOSTHENIA   Lack of strength; weakness.

IDEAS OF REFERENCE   The tendency to read a personal meaning into everything that goes on about one. Most common in paranoid individuals.

INSTITUTIONALIZATION   A bland, dependent life style which may result from living too long in large institutions that regulate day-to-day decisions and routine.

LIBRIUM   A tranquilizing medication.

LOCKED WARD   A hospital ward where entrance and exit are controlled by locked doors, the keys being held by professional and nonprofessional staff.

MANIC-DEPRESSIVE PSYCHOSIS   Prolonged periods of abnormal highs and lows in mood and behavior.

MELLARIL   A tranquilizer and antipsychotic medication.

MORAL TREATMENT   Defined by Brigham in 1847 as "...the removal of the insane from home and former associations, with respectful and kind treatment and in most cases manual labor, religious worship, establishment of regular habits of self-control, and diversion of the mind from morbid trains of thought."

OBSESSIVE-COMPULSIVE REACTION   A type of neurosis characterized by disturbing, unwanted thoughts (obsessions), and impulses to repeat previous behavior (compulsions).

OPEN WARD   One where there are no locked doors preventing movement in or out of the ward.

OT   Occupational Therapy. Usually connotes arts and crafts activities.

PAROLE   Now largely replaced by the term "ground privileges." Parole is a relatively old hospital term for designating those patients who were privileged to leave the ward and walk on the grounds without the company of an aide or relative.

PATIENT'S RIGHTS   In each state, legislation and regulations define the rights of persons hospitalized in state institutions.   Often included are the right to receive mail unopened, to make phone calls, and the right to legal counsel.   Recently, attempts have been made to define a right to treatment for involuntarily committed persons.

PERPLEXED MANIA   The patient feels "mixed up in the head" and shows a deficient grasp of the total situation in addition to exhibiting the hyperactivity characteristic of mania.

PHOBIC REACTION   A neurosis characterized by unreasonable, exaggerated, specific fear(s).

PSYCHOMETRIC EXAMINATION   Psychological assessment of intellectual performance and ability; evaluation of personality factors and emotional conflicts.

PSYCHONEUROSIS   Another word for "neurosis."   Symptoms are usually less severe than in "psychosis."   The individual's perception of reality remains intact.

PSYCHOPATHOLOGY   Any psychiatric symptoms or emotional disturbance.

PSYCHOPATHY   Long-standing character traits usually involving excitability, impulsiveness, lying, and criminality.

PSYCHOTIC DEPRESSIVE REACTION   The term for severely depressed patients who grossly misinterpret reality. Delusions, hallucinations, and paranoid symptoms may be evident.

RITALIN   An antidepressant medication.

SCHIZO-AFFECTIVE SCHIZOPHRENIA   A mixed syndrome exhibiting symptoms both of schizophrenia and of the mood disturbances found in melancholia and mania.

SCHIZOPHRENIA, SIMPLE TYPE   A chronic form of schizophrenia described by Bleuler, characterized by withdrawal, indifference to reality, isolation, blunted affect, and little apparent fantasy life.   Previously called dementia.

SCHIZOPHRENIC REACTION   A relatively severe psychosis which tends to make its first appearance when persons are in their twenties or early thirties.   Gross distortions of thinking and feeling may be present, often including hallucinations and delusions.

SERPASIL   A tranquilizer and antipsychotic medicine.

SOMATIC COMPLAINTS   Bodily symptoms. These can be caused by either emotional or actual physical problems.

STELAZINE   A potent tranquilizer and antipsychotic medication.

THORAZINE   A tranquilizer and antipsychotic medicine.

UNITIZATION   Before "unitization" large mental hospitals were divided into wards according either to the length of time a patient had been hospitalized or to the intensity of treatment attempted on the ward. When community mental health concepts became more widespread, large hospitals were reorganized so that different units received patients from different towns and communities.

VOLUNTARY   Admission to state mental hospitals is regulated by state law. If the patient requests hospitalization, the legal requirements and the hospital's obligations differ from when the hospitalization is involuntary.

WAXY FLEXIBILITY   The muscular system permits the molding of a limb into a position which then is maintained unnaturally for prolonged periods of time.

WET PACK   The patient is wrapped in wet sheets to produce both a restraining and tranquilizing effect. Such procedures are no longer practiced.